MOMMY, BE HEALED

From Loss to Restoration

Written and illustrated by
Jessica Rankin

DWilson & Associates, LLC

Photography by Lisa Owens of Now I Lay Me Down to Sleep
Back cover art painted by Kathy Tims
Copyright © 2021 Jessica Rankin
All rights reserved. Printed in the United States of America.
No part of this book may be used or reproduced in any manner whatsoever without written permission from the author.

ISBN: 978-1-7366846-3-4

DEDICATION

I dedicate this book to my husband, Nehemiah, my family, and my close friends. Thank you for encouraging me to step out in faith and write this book.
Thank you for believing in me when I did not.

CONTENTS

ACKNOWLEDGMENTS

Part 1
The Beginning of Our Lives Together 1

Part 2
Bishop Kelley Rankin 5

Part 3
The Healing Journey 19

Part 4
The Reconstruction 69

FOREWORD

BY T. RANDY ROBBINS
Hospice chaplain, retired

Jessica has written this book to offer encouragement and hope to other mothers who have lost a child during pregnancy. She is very open, transparent, vulnerable. She bares her heart and soul in the hope that you can identify with her pain and suffering and struggle ... and that you are able to find hope in the possibility that, if she can make it through all of this, you can, too.

As Jessica tells her story, she shares not only what she has experienced and endured, but she also speaks words of encouragement and shares important lessons learned along the way.

In all this, Jessica has hope for her book and for you. For her book ... that it is helpful. For you ... that, by grace through faith, you faithfully continue and successfully complete your "journey through grief" with hope in your heart and promise for your future.

As much as you are now able, be encouraged ... .

The Lord is with us!

INTRODUCTION

As I stood there next to my pastor, and he prayed over me, my mind was racing with questions. What did he just say? Did he pray that I would share my testimony in the form of written word? (Insert raspberry here.) I am not capable of something like that. Surely, not me. A book? Nah, that is beyond my capabilities… but maybe, just maybe… .

The reason his prayer had struck such a chord is because I had a dream of a book on my heart since 2010, but it was a dream that seemed too big. The mere idea of my writing a book seemed crazy. Despite this apprehension, the thought of writing would not stop tickling the back of my heart. You see, I knew I had already written this book; I had a stack of journals dating back to the beginning of my healing journey. Those journals contained all the thoughts, the feelings, the anguish, and the dark places I had struggled through — struggles chronicled in detail in 20 or so journals stuffed in my nightstand. The problem was, I had not opened those journals since I wrote them. For 10 years they sat undisturbed. The fear of what they contained kept me from opening them. I remember well the desperation, confusion, and grief I felt when I wrote them. I was scared to relive those memories. So, I avoided them. Over the years, I had thought about them often and had, on several occasions, considered burning them, but I never could. They remained a constant reminder of a dark time in my life. Or so I thought.

The word God sent through Pastor Casey that day got me to thinking. Am I capable of writing a book? Would the story written in those journals help someone? Could my story be used by God?

I knew I had experienced the healing power of God in my life. Could I share that with other people and encourage someone? I knew I had to read my journals. I knew a book was in them, but what kind of book, I wasn't sure. I gathered my courage, and I started to read the journals that I had feared for so many years. I began reading with trepidation, expecting to cry and sink into the heartache that I knew was written on those pages. To my surprise, that is not what happened. The dark anguish I was so afraid of reliving was there. The tears were there. The confusion and grief were there. But what I found on those pages full of my memories that surprised me was ... Jesus.

I saw: ENCOURAGEMENT, ANSWERED PRAYERS, HOPE, GROWTH, HEALING, AND THE WATERING OF A SMALL MUSTARD SEED OF FAITH. I cried out to God many times in those journals, and do you know what happened…?

GOD ANSWERED!

Repeatedly, He answered. I could almost touch the healing power of God in those pages. I could see all the steps of my healing journey leading me to a place of true freedom and recovery. I read the pages now and see the silhouette of Jesus holding my hand, and Him standing in the corner, and Him coming to me through His servants. I see Him in all the pages, in every memory, in every tear, in every moment of confusion and doubt, every fear, every anxiety, and every time I felt alone. I knew then, for sure, I had to write this book. I had to write this book for all the people who feel their lives are like journals filled with sad memories. I knew I had to share how God walked with me through the process of grief and how He broke the chains of unforgiveness, guilt, fear, shame, and anxiety from my life.

This book spans 10 years of my life, a small percentage of my 38 years, but in those 10 years I experienced a sharpening unlike any other time in my life. I became a wife, a mother, and finally rested in my identity as a daughter of Christ. I also became a woman who lost a child at 32 weeks gestation. Experiencing that loss was the most isolating and sad experience of my life. I felt no one understood the feelings that I was struggling with. No one could relate to the constant roller coaster of highs and lows the grief brought. Honestly, I did not understand all these feelings, either. How could anyone else?

Most of this book is taken from my journal entries dating back to 2010. I began keeping a journal the day I found out my husband, Nehemiah, and I were expecting our first child. In the beginning, it was from sheer joy that I wrote… but eventually in the wake of loss it became my place of escape and therapeutic self-care. My journals became a place to say the things on my mind that I was fearful would cause the people in my life to run from me if I said them out loud. Most of the time I was hurting when I wrote. I felt the most alone I had ever felt in my life. I hurt so deeply it seemed at times

I would never see the joyous light at the end of the tunnel. As I read my journals now, I wish I could hug the me in those pages. I wish I could tell her she is not alone, tell her there is hope, tell her grief is a process, tell her she is not crazy for feeling crazy. If you are reading this because you have experienced a loss and are grieving, or because you have chains in your life that need to be broken and healed, I pray you find solace and see your story in these pages. Know that you are not alone! I wrote this book not because my story is unique, but because my story is like so many others. During Jesus's time on earth, He healed several people in several different ways. Some He touched; some He spoke; in some instances, He used mud and spit to heal blindness. My point is your healing journey might look different, but know God is walking with you all the same. I wrote this book so you could see what I felt, so you can see that God will place ahead of you a hope so profound that no chain will be able to keep you bound.

Lord God, I pray over the person reading this book. I pray it speaks to their heart and helps to guide them to You for the healing they need. In Jesus's name, Amen.

Take heart, my friends, you are not alone,

Love,
Jessica Rankin

PART 1
The Beginning of Our Lives Together

Ten years

August 6, 2020

Dear Bishop,

It has been 10 years. Ten years have passed. Ten years since we held you. Ten years since we were together. Ten years since I felt you move in my belly. Ten years since our world changed forever. It seems like an eternity, and at the same time it seems like yesterday. So much has happened in 10 years. As I write this, your brothers are sleeping soundly in their beds. Your healthy, happy baby brothers. I'm truly grateful for the gift of your brothers, but I can't help but think of you today, son. I cannot help but to think of the milestone of reaching ten years old. What a milestone, reaching the great double digits. I also cannot help but to reflect on the path that brought us to this spot. One full of ups and downs, of sadness and of great joy. I cannot help but to be grateful for you, son. Your life may have been short, but it changed ours forever. We are thankful for the time we had with you, grateful for the gift that your life has been. It's been 10 years, but some things will always remain the same.

Mommy loves you, son, Mommy loves you

It has been 10 years since our son Bishop was born still at 32 weeks. Every day it seems more a distant memory and yet fresh at the same time. I still feel we are learning from our experience and about who the people are that we became the day he died. To understand the path, we should start at the beginning of our family.

In 2009, I married my love, Nehemiah Rankin. I had been in love with this man since we were teenagers. We meet for the first time at Harrison Central High School in Lyman, Miss. We were both 15 years old. We had history class together. He told me he knew then that we would be married someday. (He neglected to inform me of this until much later). When I was 16, I got my first job at a buffet called the Homestead. Nehemiah worked there as well. All through high school we worked alongside each other. We were friends but nothing more during those teenage years.

After graduation, I got a different job, and for a short time, we did not see each other much. In 2001, we began to hang out as friends occasionally. One night as we watched Howard the Duck, we had our first kiss. In October 2001, we went on our first date. We were both 19 years old. We have been together ever since.

Fast forward to our wedding day, April 18, 2009. The typical wedding day jitters did not plague me. I knew saying "I do" and marrying Nehemiah was the right path for my life. This is our eleventh year of marriage, and I can still say with confidence that I would say "I do" to him again. Shortly after our wedding, we purchased our first house. The house was a dream come true for us. We were excited to grow into the new space that the house offered -- space our previous one-bedroom apartment lacked. Immediately, my imagination began filling the spaces of our home with fantasies of babies and family memories. We had talked a lot about our desire to have a family, and now it seemed that all the dots were aligning perfectly. It was an exciting time in our marriage, a time full of possibilities, dreams, and hopes for a bright future.

I did, however, have some reservations about being able to have babies. I had struggled with autoimmune issues while in high school. I constantly had hives and stomach issues. Because of this, I was a bit concerned we would have a hard time getting pregnant. I decided I needed to do research and come up with a plan for becoming pregnant. This was very natural for me as I have always been an avid planner and a list maker. I think this natural tendency is rooted in my role as the older of two daughters. As the elder, I was naturally in a leadership and planning role. (My sister would call that bossy, but I prefer leadership). I have always flourished in this setting. So, I set out to educate myself on all things pregnancy: I quit smoking; I exercised; I watched my diet. I created a trusty list of check boxes to prepare myself. I then shifted into full execution mode. Part of the plan I developed was to track my ovulation. I executed this ovulation plan like a scientist would run an experiment. Every morning before getting out of bed I would take my temperature. I would make daily observations on any other physical

symptoms that could signal that I was ovulating. I kept all this data in detailed body temperature charts. I loved this whole experience. The science behind it was fascinating. The "experiment" was going well, and to our delight we discovered we were pregnant on January 31, 2010. This day marked the beginning of several things for me:

1. Motherhood
2. Journaling

The first is obvious. The minute that second little blue line appeared, I was a mother. I felt it in my heart. The second needs some explanation. I had dabbled in journaling in my youth and would write here or there. I always enjoyed writing but honestly never saw myself as very skilled at it. Despite my enjoyment of writing, I never stuck with the habit of journaling. On that day, in that moment of life change, I had to write. I had to write it down. This was a pivotal moment in our lives. Little did I know this overwhelming desire to write would have an amazing impact on my life. My first journal entry was:

Ovulated: January 7th

Found out we were pregos January 31, 2010 took 3 home tests last period Dec. 27th 2009.

Not groundbreaking or inspiring, but it marked the very beginning of the journey.

PART 2
Bishop Kelley Rankin

Then comes baby

Things progressed very well in the beginning of our pregnancy. I got set up with a midwife. I watched what I ate. I exercised. I got plenty of rest. We were enjoying the process. The next several entries in my journals are mostly notes on stretches, nutrition, baby items, recipes, and questions to ask during doctor appointments. Again, this is nothing amazing, but I was documenting my excitement. Then there are the letters I wrote to the small life inside of me. I remember writing these letters. I imagined myself reading these letters to my child later in life and reminiscing on the beginning of our lives together. I wrote these letters because my heart was so full of love for this little flicker of life growing inside me. I wrote:

Dear pookie,

Well here we are at 8 weeks. Everything seems to be going well. I can't wait to feel you move. I am so looking forward to you getting the hiccups (but not have them constantly). We go back to the doctor in two weeks. I'm not sure what to do but I am excited they will be checking on you. I feel like you are fine. I love you so much pookie. I can't wait to meet you.

Love you,
Your Mommy

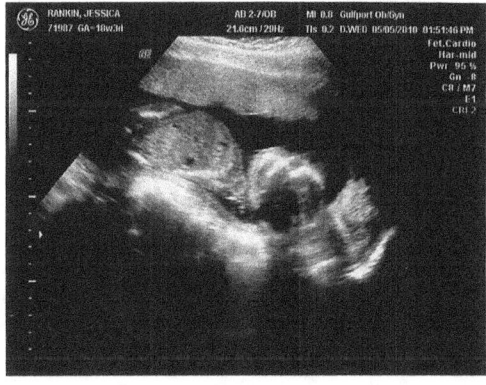

When I started reading my journals, this letter brought me so much joy, seeing how my heart was overjoyed at being pregnant. It is a blessing that I documented those moments. All throughout the pages of this first journal, I brainstormed names and made birth plans:

-I want to be mobile
-wear hospital gown
-would love music
-no medication
-natural
-no induction

I read countless books during this time, researching healthy pregnancies and deliveries. I even kept track of the number of fruit and vegetable servings I was consuming. I had shifted into super mom mode. In the early morning hours of Mother's Day 2010, I lay in the bed rubbing my little bulge. It was then that I felt it. The little flutter in my belly. The feeling of life I had been eager to feel for five months. My first-ever Mother's Day gift was the gift of movement. That little flutter was such an amazing feeling. I cried tears of joy as I enjoyed the sensation. I dreamed of the day we would meet face to face. I fantasized about all the memories we would make and all the adventures we would have as a family of three.

In June I wrote:

Dear child o'mine,

Here we are at almost six months. You are growing so fast. You are really kicking me and you are flipping and seemingly training for the Olympics. I am really starting to feel like a Mom now. I can't wait to meet you. I bet you look like your Daddy. You will be totally in love with your daddy he is awesome.

Love you,
Your mommy

This is the last letter I wrote to my child while we were still physically connected. Not long after this, all the hopes, dreams, and joy came crashing down.

At the end of July, I went to the doctor for my final ultrasound. The doctor said that the baby was measuring smaller than gestational age. We were, of course, immediately concerned. The doctor ordered a non-stress test. A non-stress test, or an NST, is a look at the baby's heart rate over a period of time to measure the health of the baby. Honestly, I was skeptical. I even spoke to

Nehemiah about how I thought they were being overly cautious. The baby was moving; surely, the baby was fine. I was scheduled to return the following week for the NST.

I went to work the morning of August 5, 2010, like I had every other day of the previous 32 weeks of my pregnancy. I left shortly before lunch to go to the doctor for the NST. I went straight to the midwife's office. Per the normal pregnancy office visit, the midwife brought in the fetal heart rate monitor. She squirted the jelly on my belly and began to roll the doppler around, looking for that familiar little heartbeat. She rolled it around and around, searching. Then this familiar practice took a turn. The midwife turned to me and said she could not find the heartbeat.

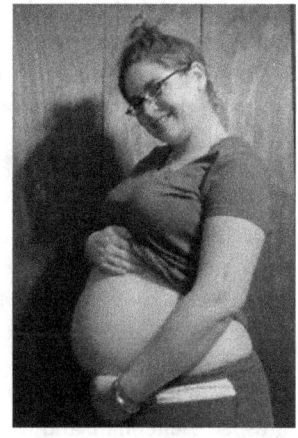

Me at 7 months

She told me I needed to call my husband. At this point I started freaking out a little bit. Was she saying something was wrong with the baby? I did not understand what was happening. Crying, I called Nehemiah, telling him they could not find the baby's heartbeat. All I remember him saying was, "I'm coming."

After I spoke to Nehemiah, I sat in the doctor's office with my mind racing. What was happening? Why couldn't she find the baby? The thought that

the baby might be dead did not cross my mind. I was confused and obviously concerned, but my mind wouldn't even consider such. As I sat crying in utter confusion, the midwife laid her hands on me and began to pray. Looking back on it now, I cannot remember what she prayed, but I remember her emotion and the comfort she offered in her prayers. She knew what was happening, even if I did not fully understand. She knew the best comfort she could offer me was from God. I am grateful she had the wisdom to pray in that moment.

The midwife said they needed to take me next door to the hospital's maternity ward for an ultrasound. To get to the hospital and avoid the other mothers, they sneaked me out the back door and along an employee hallway. I am not sure if they didn't want them to upset me or me to upset them. I can only imagine what I must have looked like. I was crying hysterically, dazed, confused, and cradling my stomach protectively. I walked along like a zombie. As we walked, my mind was struggling to make sense of what was happening. I remember the corridors seemed so long, with endless doors on either side. It was quiet, one of those quiets that compels you to say something, anything, just to alleviate it. I remember we talked, but I cannot tell you what we talked about. Eventually the maze of doors opened to the maternity ward, and they placed me in a room to wait for Nehemiah. I don't remember having any real cohesive thoughts until he arrived.

After Nehemiah arrived, they started the ultrasound. Again, they squirted the jelly on my belly. This time we had a picture as well as sound. Again, they search… and search…. We held our breath. We waited. Finally, the doctor turned to us and said, "The baby has no heartbeat." At this point I was still confused. I thought the baby was fine. So, I asked her, "What does that mean?"

To which she replied, "The baby has died." At these words, we fell apart. I grasped Nehemiah, and we cried. I did not understand. How could this be true? I had felt the baby move the day before. I remember very clearly; I was standing in my kitchen. I know the baby was alive. This cannot be true.

After an unknown amount of time, I stopped crying long enough to ask, "What do we do now?" The doctor informed us of our options:

1. We could go home and wait and see if my body would go into labor naturally. I could have the baby at home, or I could come back to the hospital.
2. We could get induced at the hospital and force my body to deliver the baby then.

We decided to go with option two. We needed to go home first, though, to get some clothes and would return later that day. We left the hospital and went back to our house, the house we had prepared for the arrival of a new baby, the house that sits baby-ready. The nursery sat pristine and ready to welcome a child. We had put the crib together the previous weekend. We pulled into the driveway, and we just sat in silence for a moment. I spoke into the silence what I was thinking, "What are we going to do?" I was at a complete loss on how to even process this. We were prepared to have a baby. How do you move forward from this? I do not remember his response, nor do I remember getting out of the car. I know we went into the house and began calling family. Family started showing up. I sat in our living room, numb…

My mom came. I remember her kneeling on the floor in front of me trying to comfort me through her own tears. I told her she should not come to the hospital. No one should go. I was worried. What if the baby had suffered? What if seeing the baby with wounds or other problems scarred us all for life? What if we could not ever sleep again from the nightmares that could plague us? I was truly afraid of these things for myself. I was truly afraid for my family. I remember well my mother's response to my fears. She said she did not care what the baby looked like, that the baby was her grandbaby and that was all that mattered. She was going, and I could not stop her. Looking back, I can see, she is a mother, a mother whose baby was suffering. All she wanted to do was fix it. She wanted to go back to the days before this and talk more of future dreams, baby names, and baby kicks. She would move whatever mountain she could to spare her child from this pain. Unfortunately, this mountain, she couldn't move, but she could walk extra close while we climbed it.

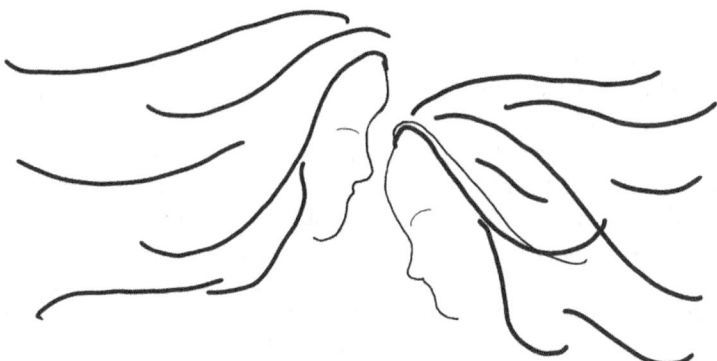

"She could walk extra close while we climbed it"

Later that afternoon, we returned to the hospital. We were admitted to a room, and the doctors began administering medicine to induce labor. Hours went by with no change. News had traveled fast in our close families, and they started arriving at the hospital to offer comfort. My mother-in-law and sister-in-law arrived soon after we got there. They came while both were processing their own grief in losing the child they had looked so forward to loving. I remember my cousin coming and painting my toenails. Another cousin comforted me when she herself had lost a son just the previous year. So many people came to love on us in our time of sorrow. This trend continues to this day. My Nehemiah and I are truly blessed to have such great family and friends who love us. Even though I was afraid for them to come to the hospital, knowing they loved us was a big help to our crushed hearts.

At one point, a nurse came in with a brochure advertising a photography company called, *Now I Lay Me Down To Sleep*. This company offered photography services for families that experience the death of a baby. The services are provided free of charge. We told the nurses we would like to use the service. The pictures they took are some of our most treasured possessions. They are the only photographs we have of our first child.

The night and the labor pains continued. My extended family started to head home. My mother, mother-in-law, and my sister-in-law stayed with us. Once it started to get a bit quiet, I began to think, "Maybe the doctors and nurses are wrong; maybe the baby will be fine." I turned to Nehemiah and asked him these questions. I remember his face so clearly, even now, all these years later. I remember the sorrow in his eyes as he just shook his head no. He did not speak, but I knew then, it was true our child was dead; the doctors were not mistaken.

As the night grew late, the doctors gave me some medicine to help me relax. I remember the beginning of contractions and doing yoga stretches that I had found during my research about pregnancy. I remember flashes of Nehemiah's face. He looked worried, lost, scared, and concerned. I pray I never see that look again. There is a reason I remember his face so vividly. It is because he stayed by my side. He tells me now that he felt like he should have done more in those moments of labor and in the months that followed. When I look back on those moments, I don't see the failure that he sees. I see us bonding in those moments, fused together in our grief and fear in those final hours of labor.

Around 3 a.m., I felt the pressure, the need to push. I told Nehemiah to get someone; something was wrong. He ran out to get help. He says he heard me yell on his way back to the room. I don't remember yelling. I remember the nurses telling me to slow down with pushing. It seemed to me that the baby was out in minutes. I remember the look of sadness on all the faces in the room. I remember the tears – no joy in this birth, no happy tears. The child we were so eager to meet was not brought into the world in a moment of happiness like I had imagined for eight months, but in a moment of grief and sorrow.

Our son,
Bishop Kelley Rankin
Born August 6, 2010, at 3:40 a.m.
2 lbs 13 ounces, 13.25 inches long

Bishop

Shortly after Bishop's birth, the photographer from *Now I Lay Me Down To Sleep* came to take pictures. The photographer came in the dark hours before the sun came up to give us the priceless gift of photographic memories of our son.

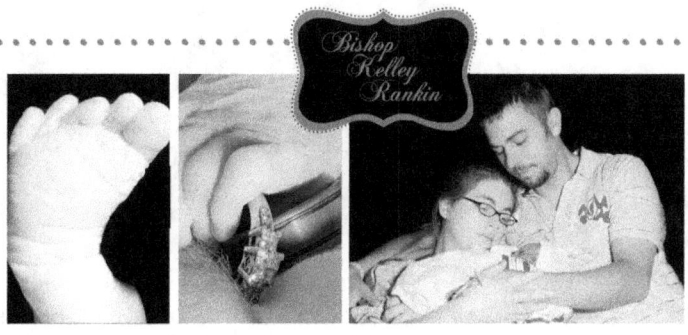

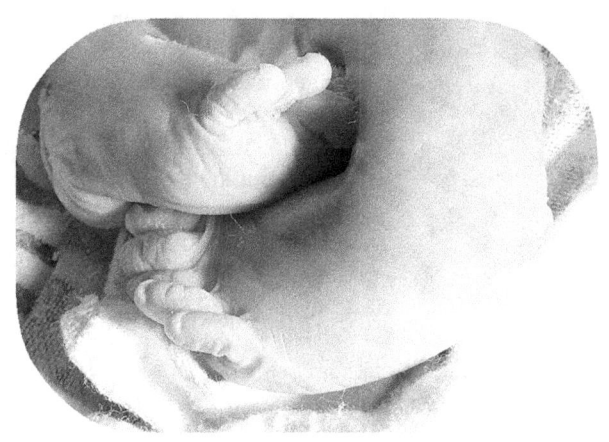

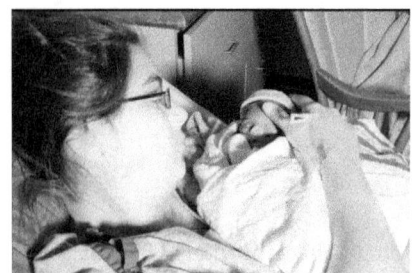
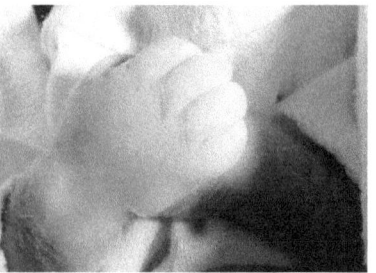
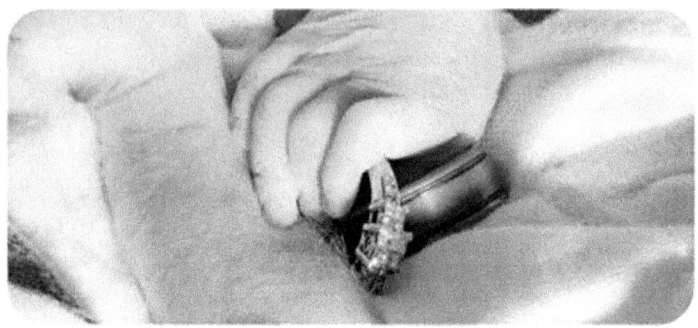

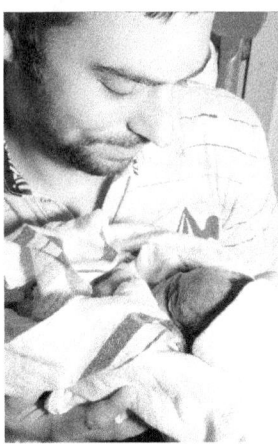
Nehemiah and Bishop

After the photo session was over, we spent hours holding him. I examined his fingers, his toes, and every inch of him. I tried to burn him into my memory. I knew I could not keep him. So, I wanted to make sure I didn't forget any of him. He was so beautiful. He was a little smaller than a full-term baby but had no obvious evidence of physical distress. The fear that had driven me to discourage family and friends from coming to see him was unfounded.

At one point in the morning, one of the nurses said that his body was getting "floppy." This absolutely crushed me. How could she say that about my baby? He was perfect; how could she say that? But she was right; his body was decomposing. My brain and my heart were not ready for that. I could not fathom being parted from him so soon. It was too soon. I thought, *"When they take him, I will never get to touch him again. What if I forget what it feels like to hold him? What if I forget his face? What if I forget what his skin feels like?"* As I write this, I am crying remembering how this felt. I felt weak, sad, and desperate -- desperate for this to all be a dream, desperate for it to all be over, but at the same time desperate for it to never end. I remember thinking, *"When he leaves, does that mean I am no longer a mother? Was I ever a mother? I felt like a mother. Did that count?"*

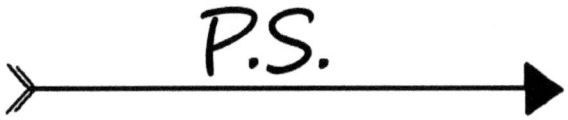

> *Just to reassure those of you in that situation, I have never forgotten what it felt like to hold him. I have never forgotten the feel of his skin. The memory of his face and the experience I had with him are forever in my heart. They will never go away. This is not an experience you get over or forget; it's one you get through. Do not be fearful of forgetting. Your child is forever part of you. You are for the rest of your life, a mother or father.*

The time had come for Bishop's body to leave us. I knew this moment was coming, but my stomach was in knots. The realization that we would never see his face in person again, the finality of it, was hard to comprehend. The nurses told us it was time to say our final goodbyes to our son. We each took a moment saying our goodbyes. Then we prayed over him. We begged God to care for our son and to help us understand. We stood over our son with our hands clasped together, weeping, crying out to God. We stood together, desperately seeking God's face in that moment, a moment when the world made no sense, a moment when we both had no idea what to do next. We made sure he knew we loved him. Then we wrapped him tightly in his blankets, and the nurse took him away. That was the last time we saw our son. His body would be returned to us after cremation as ashes.

Grief

We went home shortly after the nurses took Bishop. Back to our house with empty hands and crushed hearts. The house seemed cold, lifeless, hopeless. When we arrived home, I wondered again, *"What do we do now? How do we move forward from that?"* It is interesting now looking back on this moment, a moment of grief. My mind was racing, but it felt foggy at the same time. The grief was overwhelming.

I had not taken a shower at the hospital for fear of missing any time with our Bishop. I knew I needed to take one. I still had blood from the delivery on my legs. I was a mess. As I showered, I watched the blood flow down my legs and circle the drain. It felt dreamlike, foggy somehow, like an out-of-body experience. I wondered if this was a dream. Maybe I would wake from this nightmare at any moment and feel him kicking in my belly. The reality seemed incomprehensible. My thoughts again returned: *"What are we going to do? How can we move forward? How is this happening?"* I do not remember the rest of the day.

I remember waking in the middle of the night. All the family, the noise, the to-do lists, were gone. The only thing left in that nocturnal moment was silence. The house was quiet and still, but my mind was screaming. My thoughts were racing; my grief was crying out. I attempted to go back to bed, but my mind would not stop. I reluctantly got out of bed and sat in my empty tub. I sat and screamed and screamed over and over, silently and deafeningly, in my head. I sat sobbing, with tears pouring down my face. If I had been home by myself, I would have screamed at the top of my lungs for hours, screamed until my throat was raw. That is what I wanted to do. Knowing that Nehemiah was asleep, I screamed silently to myself alone in that dark bathroom. I screamed so forcefully I grasped the sides of my head as I rocked back and forth in my empty tub. I sat in that tub crying for hours. I sat until the sun peeked into the window. I watched the light slowly trickle into the room. I found myself not believing what I was seeing. How could the sun rise? How could this be? Surely, I am not going to continue. After what happened, life could not go on. It just did not seem right that I was still here watching the sun rise without my son.

P.S.

Physical symptoms that I battled at this stage and my recommendations:
- Insomnia - stick to a sleep schedule, exercise (if your doctor clears it), drink chamomile tea
- Food aversion - try to eat several small healthy meals, nothing too heavy (I ate a lot of sandwiches.)

Other common grief symptoms (I did not have these myself.):
- Weight loss/gain
- Fatigue
- Aches and pains

Anger

Over the next few days, my body started to do what it was supposed to do postpartum. My milk came in. This made me furious. I felt betrayed by my body. How could it function properly now and make milk? It failed to keep my baby alive, and now I am successfully making milk to feed him. I was livid. I sat in my back yard in the heat of the Mississippi summer and let the milk drip from my breasts as I cried. Every drop that drenched my shirt just made me even madder. Even looking back on it now, I remember the utter fury of this. It just seemed so unfair. It seemed like my breasts mocked me. I don't know what I had expected to happen, but I know that my milk coming in took me by surprise. Maybe I assumed that nothing worked, or maybe it was purely inexperience. Whatever the case, it was an infuriating experience for me. I had to put this pain aside as we began the funeral process for our son, Bishop.

We chose to have Bishop cremated, so we went to the funeral home that had Bishop's body. We sat and spoke with a funeral director about what we wanted to do with the ashes of our son… Our son… His ashes… I knew what I wanted to do. I wanted to run. I wanted to run away as fast as I could and not have this conversation with this man. I wanted to forget about my breasts filling with milk to feed a baby I did not get to keep. I wanted to run to a place where I chose which outfit to put him in instead of which box to put him in. It felt as if I were watching myself from the outside. The observer me was standing to the side, screaming for me to run, go back to the car, go back home, this was all a dream that would pass.

Despite all those raging thoughts, we had to choose. We had to do this. We chose a heart-shaped urn for his remains with his name and birthdate engraved on it. Together we gathered in our front yard; we prayed together, and we said goodbye to our son for the final time. I did feel some peace after the service, but it was short lived. The utter shock gave way to a range of emotions and the process of grief.

P.S.

Funeral Arrangements:

Reimann's Funeral Home in Gulfport, Miss., provided the cremation services free of charge for Bishop. We had only to purchase an urn, which was under $300. We were provided with a cremation certificate. In our case, all the ashes did not fit in the urn, so we were provided an additional box. I have never opened the box (nor will I). The urn sits on our dresser in our bedroom.

PART 3
The Healing Journey

Stages of Grief

After the funeral, I began consistently journaling to cope with what I was feeling. In some, of the journal entries, I was speaking to Bishop. In some I just wrote. In others, I spoke to God. Sometimes I wrote multiple times a day. In the first journal, I spoke mostly to Bishop. When I look back at my journals, I can see myself working through the grieving process.

In 1969, psychiatrist Elisabeth Kübler-Ross introduced her theory of the five stages of grief: denial, anger, bargaining, depression, and acceptance. She based these on her years of working with terminally ill patients. Her model is not the only one out there; there are several, some with more stages, some with fewer. It is important to note that not everyone experiences every stage, nor do they experience them in the same way, let alone in the same order. Having said that, most people do process grief through what one could call stages. I went through several stages of grief. I do not see myself mirrored exactly in the Kübler-Ross model or any model really. I do, however, see myself in a mix of several.

When I look back on my grief journey, I see these stages:

1. Denial
2. Anger
3. Pain and guilt
4. Depression and loneliness
5. Reconstruction
6. Freedom

Denial started immediately when the doctor told me our child had died. I doubted the diagnosis through my labor, so much so that I asked Nehemiah if the doctors could be mistaken. I felt the anger at my body's failure to keep Bishop safe and growing properly. I felt the fury at my breasts when my milk came in but I had no child to nurse. During the denial and anger, the pain was already going full speed with guilt fast approaching. I listed these stages from 1 to 6; however, they did not always flow in that order. My experience with grieving had no rhyme or reason. If I had to draw my journey as a diagram it would probably look something like this:

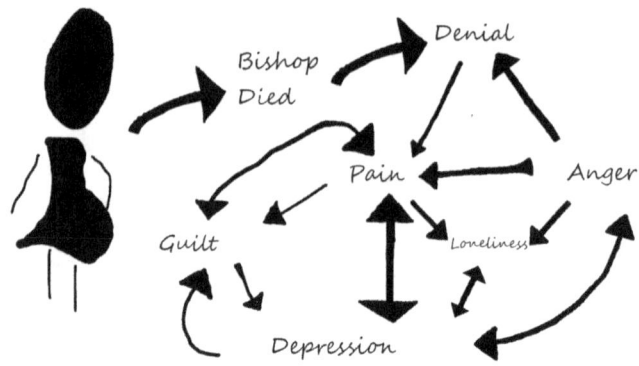

My grief was full of back tracks and swings, days full of good and days full of bad, days that should have been joyful but were tinged with sadness. Then sad days tinged with joy. I say this now, and it makes sense, the swinging. I understand it as part of the process I *had* to go through. In the middle of the stages, though, I did not see the process, only the side effects. Some of those side effects had me feeling shameful, and I felt like I should withdraw from people when really, I needed to reach out.

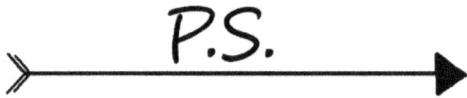

Understanding grief
　　Grief is defined as deep sorrow, especially sorrow that is caused by someone's death.
　　Grieving is defined as to distress mentally, caused to feel grief or sorrow.
　　In my research, I have found up to 10 different types of grief.
　　For the purposes of this book, here are a few that stood out to me:

Normal grief
　　As previously stated, there is no "normal grief." Think of this as any grief that is propelling you back to your state before the loss (although it will never be the same). In other words, you are on a timeline, and eventually, you will return to your normal life.

Anticipatory grief
　　As the name suggests, you are anticipating the death of a loved one due to terminal illness or situation.

Complicated grief
　　This is when the grief process gets a bit more… well, complicated. The grief you experience is long lasting, debilitating, and impairs your ability to function in daily life.

Guilt

After Bishop's funeral, I began to see the pain and guilt stage emerge in my journals. My writing took off at this point. I poured my heart out in some of these entries. I pray that by sharing them with you, they will help you with your grieving.

August 13, 2010

I'm your Mom. I should have saved you. That's my job. The only thing in life that was of the utmost importance, and I failed you. I'm so sorry Bishop. Momma is so sorry. I should have known. I should have saved you. You would have lived. I just know it.

I struggled intensely with the guilt of failing my child after his death. This guilt was a very powerful emotion for me. But what exactly is guilt? Merriam-Webster dictionary defines guilt as *feeling of deserving blame of especially for imagined offenses or from a sense of inadequacy.* This definition defines my mind set perfectly. I spent hours searching my memory for something I had done wrong, an imagined offense. I spent even more hours searching the internet looking for an answer. I just knew I had caused this, and I could figure out why he died. I was hoping we would get medical answers from the doctors.

August 13, 2010

We found out today you had genetic abnormality features. I am not sure how I feel about that. I wonder if I just hope there was a genetic problem, so I won't feel responsible. I keep thinking if I had just done a kick count that I would have saved you.

A kick count is a home test counting the number of baby kicks/movements felt in a minute.
It is widely used to assess the health and wellness of a baby, although not entirely accurate due to the differences in all of us.

I kept going back and forth in my head: if I had just done a kick count for Bishop, he would have lived. I just knew that if I had done a kick count in the days leading up to his death, I would have realized he was in distress and saved him. Looking back now, I know this would not have saved him. He did move during the days leading up to the sixth. I distinctly remember feeling him move. If I would have done a kick count, I would have felt the average number of kicks that was normal for him. I could not convince myself of this at the time, though. I was just desperately looking for answers.

I read countless articles. I read pages and pages full of comments on message boards. I searched medical websites. I read several medical journals. One day I found a message board that stated stillbirths are rare because usually mothers know when there is a problem. Those words… "mothers usually know" fell straight to the pit of my stomach. The words seemed huge on the screen, I read them over and over as I sat sobbing at our computer. Those words confirmed for me what I had feared.

I should have known he was in distress. Mothers are supposed to know when their babies are in trouble. For me, this statement justified all my guilt; it confirmed for me that it was my fault. I had no idea he was in distress, but according to the internet, I should have.

With that confirmed, I dug in even more to find out why he had died. In the coming months, I would find an answer, but looking back, I wish I had not done this to myself. At this stage in my grief, it was an unhealthy obsession. I say unhealthy because of the relentless time I spent in an almost manic state searching to find the answer. The pain of reading *mothers usually know* is still fresh in my mind to this day; the guilt was almost palpable. I would come to recognize this guilt as false guilt, but in that moment, it was the heaviest burden I had ever carried in my life. In that moment, I felt the responsibility of his death rested solely on my shoulders.

In the days and weeks following Bishop's death, I began to cry less and less and this brought on a new kind of guilt:

August 15, 2010

I only cried a little yesterday. Somehow though that upset me. Is it too soon for me to not cry all day? I feel conflicted. Part of me feels it's right, I should go on. We must survive. But part of me thinks life should not go on. I don't know.

Nehemiah and I were trying our best to get back to our normal lives. We hung with friends; we went to work; we ate dinner together.

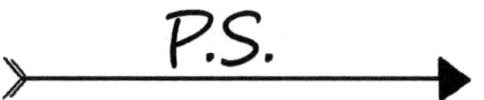

P.S.

If you find yourself in a similar manic circular pattern of obsession on anything, I recommend you take some time to journal about it. Ask yourself why you are doing this, where did it start, how do you feel when doing it, and how would you feel if you stopped. Once the obsession is uprooted and defined, it will be weaker and will have less hold on your life. If you are still struggling to control the obsession, I recommend limiting it to a specific time each day. Maybe, for example, allow yourself only 30 minutes daily.

Remember to be kind to yourself; do not let the obsession become a source of self-condemnation.

Take the opportunity to learn and grow. Identify it as a part of your grief journey, address it, respond, and then let it lie.

August 15, 2010

Nehemiah wanted to go out. I just wasn't comfortable. I'm not even sure why. I just need to be at home, I guess. I don't know. I still can't explain it. I was worried your Daddy would be a bit aggravated with me for refusing to have a good time. I've always considered myself up for a good time, but yesterday I just didn't feel right. But I don't know why. Why not enjoy myself? You would have wanted me to. I know that. I know it will help my heart heal. Maybe I just need more time. But how much time will that be?

I made what feels like a huge step tonight – I cooked dinner. Why this seemingly mundane task seems monumental, I don't know. I guess it all goes back to things I enjoy doing. I enjoy cooking for Nehemiah and me. All things I enjoyed seem far away and impossible. Maybe they should be.

After these entries, I have a note about the Women's Resource Center in Gulfport. The funeral home folks had kindly given us their contact information. The center's mission, per their mission statement, is to uphold the sanctity of life while encouraging the physical, emotional, educational, and spiritual well-being of the whole person. Its statement: "Through collaborating with organizations that share similar values, we work to promote personal health, strong family units, and thriving communities." For us, they provided counseling services. I had a positive experience in a family

My Counseling Soapbox

I *highly* recommend therapy. In my opinion it is an invaluable resource on a path to healing. Plenty of people travel through their grief journey without it, but for me, it was very helpful. I would leave each session feeling better than when I went in.

Do not be ashamed to ask for help or to speak to a professional about how you are feeling.

There are a lot of resources for counseling these days including some local churches. Trust me, friends, as they say, "It's worth a Google."

counseling session several years prior to this and knew the valuable resource counseling could be. I knew I was feeling like a complete mess at this point and decided that some counseling might help.

We began counseling before the end of August 2010. At first, we went together. We sat on the couch and explained the whole story. These counseling sessions were monumentally helpful for me. It gave me an opportunity to get the dark thoughts out of my head. We needed help, and I am forever grateful for the assistance freely given to us by the Women's Resource Center.

August 19, 2010

Today has been an exceptionally hard day. After journaling this morning, I cried especially hard. Nehemiah and I went to a counseling session tonight. I think it helped. The counselor said guilt is an emotion we should squash. I have been struggling with guilt. I felt guilty about having a good time over the weekend. I just didn't feel right having fun. But the counselor said we should have fun. I know she is right. I hope tomorrow is a better day.

One of the things the counselor and I discussed often was the guilt I struggled with. She explained to me that this was false guilt. I see, over and over in these journal entries, the guilt of moving forward. In the days and weeks after Bishop died, I cried constantly. I was deep in grief. I took three weeks off work, and even then, when I returned, I cried for weeks every day on my drive home. During that time, it was commonplace for me to look like a strawberry (I am a seriously ugly crier). I struggled with this guilt of moving forward and not crying all day again and again.

August 19, 2010

It's been two weeks since we got the worst news of our lives. My heart is still hurting. I am managing to not cry at everything anymore. All the things were making me cry, but things are getting a bit better. I put away more of my maternity clothes today without crying. It seems too soon, though, that I am not crying nonstop. The whole world seemed hopeless last week. I truly wasn't sure if I would make it. Now it seems a bit brighter; it seems too fast. Nehemiah says it is because God is with us healing our hearts. I don't know.

During my therapy sessions my counselor would remind me that false guilt is an emotion that we must squash. Life had to go on. I knew she was right, but I still struggled. We would go out to eat or go to the movies. I would enjoy myself but feel guilty afterwards. I would think, *I am supposed to be at home crying right now.* Surely I am not supposed to be out among these happy people living life like I am not dying inside. What would other mothers think? Shouldn't I be ashamed for enjoying life, when really I was feeling like I was due a punishment for failing my son? The guilt plagued me. Why did I get to live, why me? Why should I live? What entitles me to get to enjoy life? My son is dead; shouldn't I be, too?

August 25, 2010

I had a great day at work today. I am glad to be back at work. I needed to go back to work. I did feel guilty though for having a good day. I guess it seems too soon.

I carried false guilt for many years after this. The road to accepting that losing my son was not my fault, that I had done everything in my power to ensure he was safe and well cared for, was an exceptionally long and arduous road. The guilt of failing him was only one of the guilts I had.

P.S.

<u>What is false guilt?</u>

Feelings of guilt over something when you are innocent. In my case, I felt guilty over not knowing Bishop was in distress. I had no way to know this was happening. I was innocent. But I couldn't accept that in my state of grief.

Suggestions on addressing false guilt:

• Write your feelings in a journal; be descriptive. Had I done this in my grief, I imagine it would have looked something like this:

I killed my son; it was my fault that he died; I ignored signs telling me he was dying.

Had I written this, I would have seen the false in that statement. The truth is, I did everything in my power to make a healthy place for him to grow. I never missed a doctor's appointment. I did everything in my power to keep him alive.

• Focus on what you know to be true.
  - You did everything in your power to ensure the safety of your baby.
  - God has a plan and purpose for every life including your child's.

• Talk to someone. Do not keep these feelings of guilt to yourself.
  - Speak to your spouse about your feelings.
  - Talk to a close friend, preferably one who is in a good emotional place.

The Nursery

While I was struggling with my guilt, another battle was waging in my house. A week or so before we lost Bishop, Nehemiah and I completed the nursery. We put together all the furniture and hung the curtains. All the normal nesting things that a new parent does. The room was ready for a baby. It was perfect. I sat in there that week, rubbing my belly, rocking, talking to Bishop. I told him how much he would love his room. I told him about all the fun he would have playing and how we would sit and read together before bedtime. I sat and rocked and imagined all our happy times in that room.

The day we came home from the hospital, that beautiful room became a black cloud at the end of a hallway. I shut the room off, closed the door tight. I had no desire to go into that room, let alone allow someone else to go into it.

August 19, 2020

Your room is the major obstacle that I cannot take on yet. I cannot go in there. If I even think about it, I get nervous. At times I want to go in but I know that it would not go over well. I feel like I will fall apart as soon as I go inside. That room is the physical representation of all our hopes and dreams for you. It's beautiful. I could not wait to show you; you would have loved it. I love it. It's perfect, such a love-filled room. Oh, how I wish you could have seen it.

I remember battling my anger about this room. I grew to hate that room. After all the hard work and love we had put into choosing every item, I just hated it. Even with the door closed. As I said in my journal entry, it was like a physical representation of what I was considering "my failure." Every time I walked past that door, I got madder.

Remember my manic researching? I spent hours trying to find out why our son had died. Most of that searching was done in our home office. That office happened to be located directly across the hall from the nursery. Every time I went to work on my research, I walked past the room. The cursed, beautiful, perfect room.

Not going in the room did come with some issues, though. It was, after all, still a part of the house.

August 21, 2010

> *I ran into a problem today. I was going to change some lights and needed to flip the breaker, but I could not go into Bishop's room. Sometimes I want to go in, and then I think about truly going in there and I get a panicky feeling in my stomach. We cannot go in there yet. We just can't; it's too soon. It hurts too much. We worked so hard on that room and now it is just sitting idle. Mom thinks we are making it into a shrine, but I still think it is too soon. She wants to go in there to mourn. I just do not want anyone to touch anything.*

One day I reached my limit. I hated that room with such a passion, and I was going to do something about it. It had to go. I was home by myself and had looked at the closed door one too many times. I decided to take a crowbar to everything in there. I imagined myself destroying all the furniture until it was nothing but small splinters of wood. I envisioned myself screaming while I smashed it all to pieces, sweating with effort. It seemed an opportunity to take all that anger and fix the situation that the room was becoming. I wanted to smash it all, make the room into something else. Anything else!

I got the crowbar. I went to the room and opened the door. I stood and took it all in. All those hopes, all those dreams, and I just could not bring myself to smash it. Bishop never got to see that room, but to me it was still his. I just could not destroy it. I closed the door and placed the crowbar in the laundry room. It took me several more weeks before that room didn't bring me so much pain, and several more before I no longer wanted to burn it to the ground every time I walked by.

Bishop's Room

Suitable Wife?

A long with feeling like it was all my fault that Bishop had died, I also felt guilty for denying my husband his son. I was full of guilt that he had shackled himself to a barren woman.

August 27, 2010

I don't want us to be childless for life. Your Daddy, he is so fantastic, he deserves them.

Out of this guilt, fear emerged. I began to fear losing my marriage, too.

August 31, 2010

I did some research today. I read about some women that lost babies, too. One woman lost two within two years. I can only imagine how hard that would be; that makes me truly scared to ever try again. I really wanted to die a few times. I couldn't imagine losing two babies. The stories are sad. One lady had a stillborn, then her and her husband went on to have two daughters, but now they are having marital problems. She said she wonders if losing that baby has something to do with their problems now. Like her husband blames her for losing their son. That is truly scary. Nehemiah and I are good right now, but I would hate for this to cause us problems in the future. I know he doesn't blame me, but it still worries me.

Out of this fear I would over analyze our interactions.

September 7, 2010

Nehemiah was kind of quiet when I talked to him last night about why we lost Bishop. Maybe he needs a break with it. There are only so many times you can say the same thing, have the same conversation. I don't know. He seemed mad yesterday, but I am not sure. He said he wasn't, but he didn't call me at lunch, which means nothing. I am afraid that he will not want me. What if the fear of getting me pregnant will make him not want me anymore? I am probably overthinking things. I just know I want him to be happy. I need him desperately; it's kind of scary how much I need

> *him now. I feel distant and vulnerable today. I am not sure if Nehemiah is just over me falling apart. I just want to crawl into bed and cry all day. I know it solves nothing, but still I want to. Ugh. Ugh.*

I distinctly remember telling Nehemiah that in Mississippi infertility is grounds for divorce. I thought he would be better off to get out while he still could. Being shackled to me was not going to do him any favors in the kid department. When I go back and read this, what strikes me is how unfair that is to Nehemiah. How unfair that is to our marriage, really. He didn't marry me because I could provide him with offspring. It wasn't part of our vows…

"I, Nehemiah, take you, Jessica, to be my lawful fertile wife for as long as you can give me sons."

No, that is not what happened. He didn't marry me to be his baby factory. Yes, we had talked about having kids before we got married, but we never once said we would leave each other if that didn't happen. He never felt I had "cheated" him or failed him. What he understood was that we were in this together. I would always be his wife, no matter whether I bore him children or not. Having his babies is not what made me a suitable wife for him. I was a suitable wife with fertility issues. God made me to be Nehemiah's wife with my issues. He didn't marry me for what I could give him, but for what we could give each other.

Even when I did feel close to Nehemiah, my fear had me worrying about our relationship.

October 5, 2010

> *I have been feeling close to Nehemiah the past two months. I was wondering if that will hurt our relationship in the future; like it was so tense and extreme, we will suffer for it in the end. No reason to worry, I just need to make sure that doesn't happen, make an effort to keep him close, keep talking to each other.*

After reading this entry I was struck at how back and forth my feelings were in the middle of my grief journey. In one entry I am feeling lonely and distant, and, in this entry, I say we have been extra close. My emotions were all over the place. All these emotions and the multipronged guilt I was experiencing led to an inevitable by-product… shame.

Shame

I was ashamed to tell people about losing Bishop. I just knew they would look at me and know it was my fault, like I had a tattoo on my forehead that read,

MOM FAILURE. THIS WOMAN CAN'T CARE FOR HER SON

I just knew people were looking at me knowing that it was me that had caused his death. I was thinking it, so why wouldn't they? Immediately after his death, I went on the defense. First, I avoided people. I altered the paths I took to my desk in the mornings at work. I changed the direction I took to visit the restroom, all so I could avoid the conversations. If I did talk to people, I defended myself. Explaining I didn't do it. I wasn't to blame. I did blame myself, but I was so ashamed for anyone else to think that. Mostly I tried to avoid talking to people about him altogether. I spoke to close friends, but mostly avoided others. I did this for several reasons:

1. They gave me this look of pure sadness. (I don't know what facial expression they should have had.)
2. They didn't know what to say, and I didn't know what to say, either.
3. I felt the need to explain the whole thing.

Not only did I change my normal paths, I also avoided returning to places where people knew I had been pregnant. Perfect example… the pool. I swam at the natatorium near my office for a good portion of my pregnancy with my friend. We would kick back and forth across the pool and talk. It was great girl chat time and great exercise. It was time with a dear friend that I cherished. After Bishop died, I was afraid to go back.

August 27, 2010

I met with my counselor last night for a session. We talked for a while. She thinks I should go to the pool. She said it is my mountain right now, that I need to climb. I think she is right, but I am still hesitant to go. I really don't want questions, you know. We also talked about how the anticipation is way worse, and it is. I am

> *building myself up and it's probably nothing. I doubt anyone even says anything.*

In October, we decided to go back, so I prepared for any questions.

> *October 19, 2010*
>
> *We are going to start going back to the pool. I will do laps if we go back. Hit it hard. I just floated around when I was pregnant. I haven't been back since we had Bishop. If anyone asks, I just say, "I lost him," they will say, "I am so sorry," I will say, "I am too." End of discussion. See, it's easy, no worries.*

I felt my explanation made me sound crazy and guilty. At the same time, despite that, I needed to tell people; they needed to know it was not my fault. But honestly, it was because I needed to believe it was not my fault. I thought I had to convince everyone else.

During October of that year, along with walking through the grief stages, I was dreading a date that was looming on the calendar… my original due date. I knew this was going to be a particularly difficult day for me. It was the day I had dreamed of for months, the day I was supposed to meet our child, the day we were supposed to become a family.

> *October 1, 2010*
>
> *Sunday is my due date. I was supposed to be fat and happy today, about to have a healthy, happy, full-term baby. Here I am struggling to keep my sanity in the wake of losing him. I miss my Bishop so badly. I just want my baby back. I want to be in the hospital with labor pains. I guess it truly doesn't matter what I want. I am in control of nothing. I looked at his baby book last night. I still feel like this is all not really happening. It all seems like a dream. It feels some days like I was never pregnant. Did I dream the whole thing? It makes me confused. I wonder if it's my brain protecting me, but that doesn't make any sense because I have been upset for weeks, months. I wonder how bad it could be if I am protecting myself. I don't think that's the case. It's just surreal, I guess.*

> *October 3, 2010*
>
> *Today was our due date. We should have a beautiful baby boy with us right now. But that is not what happened. Me and Nehemiah are alone chilling at the house. I miss my baby.*

This day was a tough day. I kept imagining myself with him, smiling down at him, breastfeeding him, or rocking him to sleep. This day was tough, but there were more tough days to come.

Anxiety

Another fun little emotion born from my pain and guilt was anxiety. The anxiety began with Bishop's ashes. As I said earlier, we had Bishop cremated, and we purchased a heart-shaped urn for his ashes. We placed Bishops' heart-shaped urn on our dresser near a stuffed monkey that my great-grandmother had sewn for him before he died. Every time I left the house, I placed the urn in our fire/waterproof safe. Once I returned to the house, I would place it back in its assigned place on the dresser. Now, that doesn't sound all that bad, right? I mean, it is his "grave," so it should be treated with respect.

But it was not out of respect that I was moving the urn. It was out of obsession. My heart was full of anxiety that something would happen to those ashes. I worried over endless what-if scenarios. What if the house caught on fire? I devised a plan of escape, taking the urn with me when I ran from the flaming house. I conducted mock fire drills in my head. What if we had a flood? I devised a plan to keep the urn with me in case of excessive rain. But the one that really worried me was what if someone broke into my house and stole the safe? This was the peak of my anxiety. The place I was relying on to keep the urn safe now seemed unsafe. My stomach ached with the anxiety of protecting the urn.

One morning, shortly after I had gone back to work, I noticed our side gate was left open. Now this was probably an oversight by me or my husband when we used the water hose. In my anxious state, I envisioned an entire insidious plot to break into my house perpetrated by a professional thief. What if that person came back? What if they break into the house while I'm at work? What if they steal the safe? I was so worried, I contemplated taking off work to guard the urn. I stood in my bedroom and cried, contemplating whether I should stay home or go to work. In my head this wasn't just me leaving an urn full of ashes, it was me abandoning my baby. I thought that if that urn was stolen, I would fail him again. I knew I needed to address this. I knew being too anxious to leave the house was a red flag.

I talked to a friend about my anxiety, and they said that I was justified in my feelings. The ashes of Bishop were all I had left. So, of course, it made sense for me to feel anxious about losing them. Here is the thing, though: it was beginning to cripple me from living. Yes, his ashes were all we had left of him physically. But I couldn't live my life guarding ashes as if they were a live baby, which was exactly what I was doing. That day, I made myself leave my house. I had to make the decision to leave. I had to make that decision *every day* for months before I could overcome the anxiety. I was eventually able to lay this anxiety down, *but* I picked up new ones. The problem was, I did not recognize them like I did the obsession over the urn, and the new anxieties influenced my life for many years.

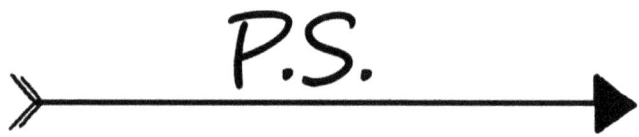

What is anxiety?

The dictionary defines anxiety as a feeling of worry, nervousness, or unease, typically about an imminent event or some uncertain outcome.

Anxiety in psychology is defined as a nervous disorder characterized by a state of excessive uneasiness and apprehension, typically with compulsive behaviors or panic attacks.

My thoughts on anxiety:

Sometimes anxiety masks itself as rational. As if it were necessary for me to worry. If I didn't worry over it, I was in some way acting irresponsibly. I am sure in reading that, you can see the falsity in that statement. If you find yourself feeling anxious, ask yourself why you feel this way and what you can do about that thing. If you can't do anything about it, pray about it, then lay it down. You will have to keep making the decision to lay it down, but continue to do so. In my situation I had to lead with my decision to the leave the house; eventually, my feelings followed.

Depression

During my pain and guilt stage, I began to see depression and loneliness emerge. My depression was not diagnosed clinical depression. I have friends who battle clinical depression, and what I experienced was *not* that. My experience with depression was not a medical condition; it was a period of depression because of grief. If you are battling clinical depression, I encourage you to seek help. Please do not take my experience as what an individual with clinical depression would experience.

With depression and loneliness starting to set in, the anxiety of trying again to have a baby weighed heavily on me.

October 4, 2010

Nehemiah and I talked the other day and we decided to try again next year for a baby. I love this plan; it makes sense to me. When I go to the doctor, we can see where we are on the health issues, see if we are super high risk. If it's too high of a risk, maybe we could adopt. We will just have to see.

October 6, 2010

Maybe I should go home today. I really want to cry today. I could go home and clean the crap out of anything and everything. This will only make the house clean and use a day of leave. I should stay at work and concentrate, even though I just want to cry.

I NEED TO STAY AT WORK
I CAN'T GO HOME TO AN EMPTY HOUSE AND CRY
IT IS HEALTHIER TO WORK
I WILL FEEL WORSE AT HOME
YOU CAN DO IT!!!

October 7, 2010

I am so lonely today. I want a baby terribly. I don't know why I want a baby for us so badly. We are going to rearrange the house this weekend. We are putting the computer in the den and change the office into a guest room. I was thinking the reason I didn't want to make a guest room is because I wanted to fill that part of the house with babies. That seems to be easier said than done. I guess now I feel like I may never need that room. I want to leave the nursery alone. Why change it, we may need it in 2012. That seems like a long time away, but it isn't. I have no desire to do anything with that room. I want to put a baby in it or maybe two.

I do feel good about waiting to try again. I mean, we must for health reasons. I wonder if we would have waited a couple more months if the outcome would have been different; I mean, maybe that egg and sperm would have had a better chance. I don't know and really it doesn't do me any good to wonder. The 'what ifs' are a waste of good brain power.

2012 is not that far away. Maybe we will be pregnant by next Christmas, then be blessed with a beautiful child, or maybe we will get lucky and have 2. That would be scary but awesome. I would be scared for the babies. I am already scared. Women that have had stillborns are more likely to have another. That is a terrifying concept. My heart is already broken. I don't think I could live through another loss.

Thank God I have Nehemiah. I wouldn't be able to stomach this loss without him. I know the yearn for a baby would be even worse. I think I just must work through these feelings. We will have a baby one day. I will be able to hold our child and watch him/her grow into a beautiful adult. I just have to wait a year.

October 18, 2010

I have been plagued the past few days with thoughts of lifelong childlessness. I guess maybe I feel I should embrace it, because maybe it's inevitable. Maybe I shouldn't get my hopes up. I was thinking about it and yeah, I guess I just want to prepare myself for a childless future. I wonder why. I wonder if my subconscious knows something I don't. I guess I feel gun-shy, like if I keep telling myself, "Hey, we may never have kids, just embrace it and move on, enjoy being an adult," maybe then I won't feel so shitty about being childless. My friend hasn't wanted to walk lately. I wonder if it is because I am bad company. My conversations are depressing and should be reserved for a therapy session not an exercise that is meant to be relaxing. I just ramble on and on when we walk about missing my Bishop and being heartbroken. She doesn't need to hear it. I feel like I am not being a particularly good friend. I am scared I will push her away with all these emotions.

So now that it has been a few months, all the mothers I knew *that were pregnant at the same time as me have had healthy babies. I am happy for them, but honestly sadder for me. Why did I have to be the 1 in 200 to have a stillbirth? When will I get my healthy baby? Will I ever get one? Will these questions ever stop haunting me? Will they stop ruling my thought process?*

October 23, 2010

Nehemiah said this morning he didn't want to put a time limit on it (baby making). I am not sure what that means. I said we should try in a year; he said he thought we shouldn't put a limit on it. I don't know if that means sooner or later. I don't know. I need to talk to him about it again. I know I feel on the fence about the baby thing. I'm scared, then not; I never want to be pregnant again, then I can't wait. I feel like a crazy person most days. It really sucks. All this back and forth and endless questions.

The Diagnosis

As I discussed earlier, in August I began the relentless, exhaustive, unhealthy search to figure out why Bishop had died. During that time, I did manage to stumble on what I thought was a probable cause, antiphospholipid syndrome (APS). According to the Mayo Clinic, this syndrome causes a person's immune system to create antibodies that make their blood much more likely to clot. The clots can lead to miscarriage or stillbirth. With my symptoms and having had autoimmune issues when I was in high school, this seemed a probable cause to me.

After I discovered the possibility of my having APS, I began doing research on having a baby. There was plenty of research on women with APS having successful pregnancies with the aid of blood thinner medication.

Despite my desire to have a baby, I was terrified for the same thing to happen twice.

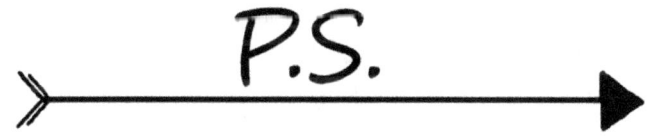

{ According to the Mayo Clinic, antiphospholipid syndrome occurs when your immune system mistakenly creates antibodies that make your blood much more likely to clot. This can cause dangerous blood clots in the legs, kidneys, lungs, and brain. In pregnant women, antiphospholipid syndrome also can result in miscarriage and stillbirth. }

October 25, 2010

I have been so busy today. I am having a good day, feeling good. I guess because it has been almost three months. I do have to go to the doctor soon to see what is going on with the APS situation. Even though I have no desire to make a baby right this minute (not only my body but also my mind isn't ready), I do really want to know where we stand. If I have APS then maybe I could find a good doctor to help when we do get pregnant again. I talked to Nehemiah about what he said the other day about not wanting a time limit on it. He said he just wants to take it easy and see what happens. I agree with him. I do want to get off birth control in a few months. I want none of that in my system when we decide to get pregnant. I think once we are out of the danger zone, we could stop trying not to get pregnant and just see what happens. I hope the doctor can set us straight and give us some advice on what to do. I do wonder if I am talking about all this baby stuff too often. I don't think it is possible for me to not talk about it. I am a planner. I like to know at least where we stand.

What if I get pregnant again and I lose that baby? There are times now that I just want to die. I couldn't imagine doing this again. I don't know; I guess I should just stop thinking about it. What if I am too old? What if I waited too long? I want to be a mommy. I want a baby. I am Bishop's Mom, but I still want a baby to cuddle and love, teach, etc. I do think that I need some more counseling. I have felt sad for weeks now, a heavy sadness that makes me want to just lay in bed and cry all day. I want to cry now. I am a bit nervous about Nehemiah thinking, "Well why do you need more counseling?" Why be constantly sad? I feel terrible today. I guess it's just a bad day. I'm allowed to have them. I know that, but that doesn't make them any easier. I can't write anymore; I am too emotional today.

On October 27 I went to the doctor to be tested for APS. This was a critical appointment. I thought a diagnosis of APS made sense with my symptoms, but I had no official diagnosis.

October 27, 2010

I am going to the doctor today, so I am nervous about that. I need to be able to talk there and not cry the whole time. What if I don't have APS, then what do we do? If I do have APS, how will that make me feel? I caused my Bishop's death. Not on purpose, but maybe I could have saved him. What if this changes Nehemiah's perception of me, if we find out my body killed our son? I know Nehemiah loves me and wouldn't want to be upset at me, but it could fester deep down. Maybe I am crazy. I had no idea.

I didn't know; how could I have known? Ok, calm down. I am getting all worked up, and I may not have APS. I may be fine; it could be a genetic fluke. Blah, what a horrible spot. Lord, please help us.

Later that day:
3:00p.m.

OK, here I am at the doctor's office seeking answers to a question I am not sure I want answered. This whole situation sucks. I hate it! But playing the woe-is-me card won't help. It won't do me any good. God, I hope this doctor listens to what I have to say. I hope it gives me some ... well ... some something.

October 28, 2010 – the next day

The doctor appointment went so well. He sat and talked with me for almost an hour. He listened to everything I had to say. I even asked some questions that had the same answers, and he was really patient. The most important thing he said was that we could get pregnant again after three normal periods. I was happy to hear that. Waiting a year seemed so far away. I guess putting a number on it made me feel so hopeless. I like that we don't have to wait a certain amount of time. I am not ready this month to get pregnant, but maybe I will be in a few months. Who knows? I did have the APS test run. He did say it could have been a random genetic problem. He said since we don't have any genetic issues in the family, he thought maybe cord strangulation could have been the  *cause. He said this is the leading cause of stillbirth. We didn't get the genetic testing done. I am a bit worried that if we get pregnant again, and (God forbid) we lose the baby, then I will never forgive myself for not getting the test. But $1,000 is a lot of money, and we may find out nothing. Our odds are low since genetic issues don't run in our family.*

November 5, 2010

My doctor called last night. I was diagnosed with APS, a blood clot disorder. So now we know what happened to Bishop. My "toxic uterus" killed him. That reads so nasty. I don't feel responsible. I didn't know. I couldn't have known. I wish I had. My Bishop would be alive and well. I am mad/sad that my baby could have been saved. He was perfect! He just didn't get enough "juice" from me. That makes me sad. I wish he were here. Now I am scared to be pregnant, even knowing it can be prevented. We can save one. For some odd reason it does my heart good to know that he was perfect. His mommy just couldn't pump enough blood for us. Even knowing something can be done about it next time, I am still scared. I don't know if my heart can take it. I don't think Nehemiah's heart can take it. Can we take two losses or more? I knew it was the APS thing, I knew it. I'm so sorry, Son; Mommy didn't figure it out before now. I'm sorry you had to die because of it. I hope your Daddy can forgive me. I love you, Son, so much; please know I would have given my life to save you without a single thought.

I remember how I felt in that moment. I remember writing "toxic uterus." I remember feeling utterly lost, confused, and filled with shame. I was scared to move forward, but I was also scared not to. This was the most confusing time in my life. I was coming down from the utter shock of losing Bishop into resuming life, but I was still emotionally struggling. My everyday thoughts were consumed by guilt, shame, depression, loneliness, anxiety, and the fear that I would lose the people I had left.

Try Again?

It was a time of decisions that could affect the remainder of our lives. Do we try again? Do we place ourselves in that vulnerable position, a position that utterly terrified me and filled me with hope at the same time? I placed a lot of my November 2010 journal in this book for you to read. I wanted you to see the emotional ups and downs in this period of uncertainty. I admit I was apprehensive to share all these writings because of how real they are, but that seemed even more reason to share them. As I read them, I am struck at how the grief process and the battles within it were manifesting in my life.

After I got the news about the diagnosis, I had a lot of questions.

November 8, 2010

My doctor called me back today; he made me feel better about the blood clot disorder. I was worried about being a walking time bomb for blood clots. He said I am only at a slightly higher risk than the normal population. The success rate for pregnancies treated with blood thinners (aspirin and heparin) is 70-85%. So, those are pretty good odds. I think Nehemiah feels better knowing. We stopped taking birth control and we are going to see what happens. Thank you, Son, for making me truly understand the frailty of life. Thanks for making us better parents.

Lord, please help me to see our many blessings and please bless us with a healthy child. Give us strength to try again. Please watch over my family and look over my Nehemiah.
Amen

With the doctor's reassurance that we could have a healthy baby, we stopped taking birth control. I wanted to try again, but honestly, I was terrified and confused. I knew I wanted to have a baby, but I didn't think my heart could take another loss. I began tracking my ovulation again, took my temperature every morning, ate right, and began exercising. Fear and uncertainty were constant companions for me. I was still struggling with the guilt and shame. These two companions of mine would manifest in my life in surprising ways. I had terrible self-esteem. Why should anyone see me as anything when I didn't see myself that way? Every conversation, every moment was assessed through a lens of self-doubt, and honestly, self-hatred. I constantly looked for any sign of people being upset with me or of my failing at something again. All my interactions and experiences were run through the filter of the emotional roller coaster I was going through. When you are rooted in unforgiveness and looking at your life through the unforgiveness filter, even good things have a hard time reaching your heart.

November 12, 2010

Yesterday was a holiday. I stayed home for most of the day. I was super lonely. I need to shake that. I guess I feel like a mommy without a baby. So now I am lonely when I am by myself. I was always comfortable with myself, but now I am not. I am just lonely. I miss my baby. I am not supposed to go shopping all by myself. Bishop is supposed to be with me crying, causing me problems. That would be great. Nehemiah and I decided to let the baby schedule just happen. I feel better about that. There isn't a schedule. I feel good about it, although I must admit that now seems very soon. I am kind of hoping it takes a while. But that makes me feel guilty. I should feel blessed for whatever time it happens. I am still super scared and still really want my Bishop more than anything.

November 15, 2010

Lots happened the past week or so. I have been super swamped at work, which is a blessing. I haven't had much time to think except for the holiday that I was home by myself. That is not a good idea. I need to be around people. Otherwise, I am just lonely. So last night I talked to Nehemiah about being scared to get pregnant now. I don't want to right now. I feel bad for saying it. If I get pregnant, I would be happy (I think). I am wondering how I will feel in the next pregnancy. What if I don't bond with the baby because it's not Bishop? I don't know. On the days that I can just not worry about it, I feel great. But I am truly worried about not bonding with the baby. I should be able to bond. I was over the moon about Bishop. Surely, I will feel the same about another baby. I just don't know. I was so in love with Bishop, I felt like his mother. What if I get pregnant and parts of me just really want to have a boy? Is that just because I lost a boy? I need to be happy with either gender. But I don't know if I can. I know my heart wants a boy. I know I can't replace my Bishop, he was one of a kind. I need to stop worrying about this. The "what ifs" are not helping. I bet I will bond with another one just like I did with Bishop. We will see when we get there.

I struggled with the notion that the only reason I wanted to get pregnant again was because I wanted to "replace" Bishop. I felt guilty even having those thoughts. I struggled to truthfully examine my motives for wanting to have another baby. Did I just think I could replace him? Did I genuinely want to have a child, or did I just want to replace the one I had lost? With these questions swirling in my head, I kept questioning whether I could love another child. I worried I'd expect the new baby to be a Band-aid (if you will) to stop my heart from aching constantly. Once the novelty wore off, I would not love the baby. These thoughts had me questioning whether I should even be a mother.

November 16, 2010

I was thinking on my way to work, what if I am pregnant now. But I don't really feel pregnant. It may still be too soon. I had a little bit of disappointment about that this morning. What the hell is wrong with me? I didn't want to be pregnant yet. Now here I am upset because I am not pregnant. This makes no sense. I am just… crazy is what it is. I am a maniac. I hope no one ever reads this, they would really think I am nuts.

Not lost on me is the irony of my writing "I hope no one ever reads this," when ten years later I am typing those words into a book, a book that I pray people read and find comforting. Life is crazy and amazing.

November 19, 2010

I felt my belly last night and it feels kind of funny. What if I am pregnant? I shouldn't tell anyone. They will just think I am crazy, mourning for Bishop and trying to replace him. I know I can't replace him. Having another baby won't make me any less sad for my Bishop. I miss him terribly. I can't ever get him back. I feel like we had a special bond. I am so scared I will not bond with another baby. I am terrified. What if I am too scared to open my heart to another pregnancy?

We went to Target yesterday. They had some 'baby's first Christmas' stuff. It made me want to cry. I should be buying that stuff. I am still tempted to buy him stuff. That is not an option. He isn't here. I think that would make me crazy. I always want to buy him stuff, I guess, because I am still his mommy and I love him. I have a couple of friends having babies. I should buy something for them. I do want to be supportive. Honestly, they make my heart ache a little. It is getting better though; pregnant women don't make me as sad as they did.

My feelings toward pregnant women were a mix of sadness and jealously. I longed to still be where they were, filled with child and awaiting my due date. It seemed like now that I wasn't pregnant, I saw expectant mothers everywhere I went. I would cringe inwardly when I saw one, knowing the wave of emotion that would follow. I always felt bad that pregnant women made me sad. But since this journal entry, I have spoken to several other women who experienced similar feelings. They also felt bad about feeling that way. If you are feeling this way, remember you are not alone. With time, you will look upon those pregnant ladies with affection instead of sadness or jealously.

November 30, 2010

Thanksgiving came and went. I knew that day would be sad, and it was. I cried when Uncle Ron blessed the food. I ran outside, though I didn't want to black mark the dinner. I was feeling sad that Bishop wasn't there. I think I have transitioned from missing the baby to missing Bishop. I know that reads weird, but that's how I feel. I think that's a good thing.

Been thinking about if we get pregnant soon. What if, even with blood thinners, the baby still doesn't get enough blood from me. I don't want the baby to have issues because of me. What a crappy situation. Maybe we should adopt. I should talk to Nehemiah about it. My life seems so crazy right now. I always knew Nehemiah and I would get married; I knew we would have kids. But now I am not sure about anything. That makes me sad and confused. My life feels like it is in limbo. Lord please help me find peace.

> I told Nehemiah last night maybe we should do something with the baby room. Maybe we should take down the furniture. I have no desire to do anything with the room. I guess we should just leave it. I don't know. I just looked at some pictures from when we were pregnant. It seems so far away, like it never happened, like it happened to other people, not us. It seems sometimes like I was never pregnant. It is weird. I don't understand it. I told Nehemiah these past 4 months have been the longest and hardest of my life.

> December 2, 2010

> Today is December 2. My period is late. I am going to take a pregnancy test tonight. I can't take it anymore. I must know. I know I need to just not worry about it, but I just cannot. It is all I can think about. I hope Nehemiah is excited if we are. I know he is not ready yet. I know he is scared. I am too. I am terrified; I am so scared the same thing will happen.

Despite my period being a little late, I was not pregnant. I admit I was disappointed when I would take a test and the result was negative, but then I felt those conflicting emotions of not feeling ready to be pregnant.

Letter to Bishop December 3, 2010

> My dearest Bishop,
> Mommy misses you so much. I miss you kicking me. I miss you. I just miss you. I dreamed of you the whole time we were pregnant. I miss you terribly. But now I know, Son, you would have struggled in life. We still would have loved you so much, but I would not have wanted to see you suffer. We will meet again one day in heaven. Until then, my sweet angel, know that Mommy and Daddy love you so much and will for the rest of our lives.
> I love you son. Mommy loves you

> December 9, 2010

> Ya think when I run out of stuff to complain about that I am all healed. I guess not. I don't think I will ever truly be healed. My heart will be broken forever. Even when we do have another baby. I will have an empty spot for my Bishop. This Christmas will always be the Christmas that would have been his first Christmas. He should be in my arms not really caring about all the Christmas stuff.

I remember my frustration with myself during that holiday season. Why can't I just feel better? Why can't I just be happy again? As you can see in the entry from the ninth, I kept wondering when it would stop. I have seen this in others' walk through grief as well. As if we keep ourselves on a limited time budget for the stages of grief. I was less than five months out from losing Bishop, and I was already condemning myself for being sad too long. There is a point when we must move forward, but there is also a time to grieve. Friends, please remember to be kind to yourself. As you will see in the next chapter, you are worth that kindness and so much more.

> December 14, 2010
>
> *Nehemiah had a great idea to make a stocking for Bishop. I am excited about it. I think I have been struggling because I was so looking forward to this Christmas. Last Christmas I was looking forward to this Christmas. I had it all dreamed out. I have been struggling with those dreams not being a reality. I just want to go home and cry. Such an awful idea. That won't make me feel better. I have stuff to do today. I don't have time to lay in bed all day and cry. I don't want to be sad about Christmas. I don't want to ruin everyone else's Christmas.*
>
> *I've discovered that only imagining him in my mind brings me any comfort now. I was finding some comfort in his blankets and stuff, but they don't help now. They are just things — things he never touched. The hospital blanket that did touch him was cremated with him. I couldn't bear to unwrap him in case he got cold. I doubt even that blanket would bring me comfort now. All I have is his Daddy.*

We did make a stocking for Bishop that year. I bought two wooden cars, and my family wrote letters and placed them in the stocking. This stocking was a great comfort to me on that Christmas. I think it was for my family as well. It acknowledged him, and that helped me that Christmas.

My letter I placed in his stocking that first Christmas.

> *My Baby Boy,*
> *Tonight, is Christmas Eve. Tonight, Santa comes. We made you a stocking because we love you desperately. I miss you my love. Mommy loves you so much.*
>
> *Merry Christmas Baby,*
> *Mommy loves you*

Self-care

In the new year of 2011, I decided to take up a hobby (aka, being kind to myself). With all the back-and-forth mental struggles, I knew I needed a distraction. A woman at work started a couch to 5K running program. If you are not familiar with this program, it is a six-week schedule that builds you up from no running (couch) to running a 5K (hence, the name). Running was never something I saw myself doing, but I figured, "Why not?" I was fully entrenched in a season of doing things I never thought I would do. I did enjoy walking, especially with friends, so it seemed worth a try. To my surprise I happily discovered that I enjoyed running. I found it to be a much-needed mental break from the normal hamster-wheel thought process I was fighting. My body's working would drown out my mind screaming in grief. Finishing that 5K became my goal. I was diligent in my training, mostly because I needed it. Also, my running buddy was so encouraging. She would run with me and speak encouragement over me. God bless this woman, because I was in a dark place. I am positive I was not enjoyable company, but she stayed with me. She trained with me and ran the 5K with me, speaking encouragement the entire time. I have since run countless miles, races, and even completed a marathon in 2018 (which was one of the hardest things I ever did, up to this point, but it was one of my favorite accomplishments). It all began with the couch to 5K. I have continued to find peace in running. The wind in my hair, my legs yelling at me to stop, the feeling of pushing my body to do things I didn't think were possible. Running was the healthy thing I needed in that moment in my life.  The friends I have made since those first training runs have had major impacts on my life. The health and sense of accomplishment I have gained by pushing myself in training and in races have served me in all aspects of my life.

I think one of the reasons running was healing for me was because of the lens in which I was viewing my body in that season. Remember my anger at my breasts for producing milk when my womb would not protect my son?

Well, running was the outlet I needed to feel physically capable again. My body could and would do things. It was not a "busted" shell, so to speak. The marathon I ran in 2018 was one of the hardest things I have done physically. Those twenty-six miles were a grueling test of mental and physical strength for me. On the other side of it, I know that physically there is not much I can't do. My body is wonderfully made.

I am not suggesting that everyone take up running (my sister absolutely hates running, despite my attempts at convincing her otherwise), but I am recommending you find yourself a "thing." Find something that is about your being kind to you. To assist you in finding a thing, let's look at the fine details of my thing.

Me on the final stretch of the Mississippi Gulf Coast 2018 Marathon

Running (aka, my thing) offered me:
1. Time to appreciate the strength of my body.
2. Time to be outside in the fresh air doing something physically healthy.
3. Time to focus on something other than the grief.
4. A friend to speak encouragement over me.
5. Relatively low monetary investment (first race cost $18; subsequent larger races have gotten more expensive).
6. A challenge mentally and physically.

Thinking along this mindset, I believe the possibilities are endless. Is there something you have always wanted to try? Basket weaving? Crochet? Parkour (I would personally love to do this one, but I am not very graceful and would probably fall straight on my face trying to jump a curb)? Bicycling? Kayaking? Skating? Fishing? The list goes on and on.

Keep in mind, when choosing a thing for yourself, you should consider it self-care. As women, we all too often

Nehemiah and I after I completed the marathon

sacrifice our self-care. We are nurturers and tend to worry about the health of others before ourselves, but we aren't doing anyone any favors neglecting ourselves. I am sure you have heard the expression, "You can't pour from an empty cup." Well, it's true. How are we to care for others, if we will not care for ourselves? Author, speaker, and pastor, John Maxwell, often says the hardest person to lead is yourself. I believe this. I have often thought the hardest person to care for is yourself. A lot of us want to put ourselves last, to sacrifice for the betterment of others. While a humble servant attitude is one of the keys to success, we must care for ourselves as well. Part of the healing journey for me was to care for myself and pour into my cup, give myself permission to do something just for me. Running was all about me and challenging myself. It was about working on me, physically and mentally. It was all about self-care.

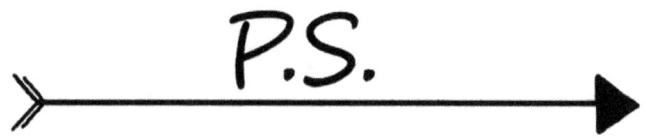

Suggestions to help you find a life-giving "thing":
- Physical activity such as walking, running, swimming, yoga, etc.
- Gardening
- Painting
- Macramé (I have recently started this, and it's surprisingly fun)
- Join a Bible study group (there are lots of online options now; video conference with a group. Find some options here: https://northwood.church/smallgroups

Baby #2

Nehemiah and I continued our conversations about having another baby, and at the start of the new year, it was at the forefront of my mind. I continued to wonder whether the grief would ever stop. Did I think a new life would bandage all the emotions I was struggling with? Maybe I did. Maybe I assumed the romanticized thoughts I was having about the life we lost could be repaired with just inserting another person. I remember the desperation I felt in those months of not knowing if this would be the month. I remember the disappointment when my period would come. I began keeping track of my basal body temperature to pinpoint my ovulation calendar. Just like when we were trying to have Bishop, I found it a very enjoyable task. I would take the temperature and add it to graphs I was creating. The day when my body temperature would fall slightly would indicate ovulation the following day.

Luckily not far into the year, we found out we were expecting. Of course, we were overjoyed, but fear came instantly, the thoughts of a repeat of the previous year played over and over in my head.

March 17, 2011

Its 5:07 a.m. about 20-30 minutes ago we learned we are pregnant!!!! O.M.G. I am so excited. I took a test on day 30 of my cycle and it was negative, I guess it was too soon. I am freaking out; I can't believe this. God please please please please please bless us with a healthy baby this year. Amen. Woohoo I am super stoked. Now I need to call the OBGYN. I am doing the 5K on Saturday, but I will be fine because I have been doing it. I will not be overworked. I am really excited about it. I have been watching my calories. I better stop doing that. I will call the doctor and make an appointment. I will also ask him about the running.

As soon as we found out we were expecting, I was eager to see the doctor. I knew we were going to need the blood thinner therapy because of my APS diagnosis. I practically ran there as soon as I could.

March 18, 2011

We told our mothers last night. They are excited. Mom cried. Nehemiah was tired, so he was not too excited about the whole thing. I know he is happy. I guess it's just a lot to take in. We talked a little about how it's weird that we are pregnant with a completely different person. It is not Bishop. It is kind of messing with our heads a bit. I wonder if that will go away once I feel the baby kick. I can't wait for that. Bishop moved on Mother's Day in the 5th month. The 5th month with this baby is in June. Maybe I will feel the baby move on Nehemiah's birthday.

As excited as I was about being pregnant again, I was truly terrified. The "what ifs" were really weighing on me. What if I lose the baby again? What if the blood thinning medication doesn't work? What if they get my dosage of medicine wrong, and this is all a set up for failure again? What if I am just not capable of safely carrying a baby? What if I place unrealistic expectations on a baby to make my heart stop aching? At the top of the list of questions was one that kept playing at the back of my mind. The question that terrified me. What if we lose this baby, and I cannot survive it again? What if the baby dies, and my heart literally breaks? I was truly afraid I was not strong enough to go through that again. I was afraid I would go crazy if I found myself there again. With all that on our minds, we were at first apprehensive about telling people of the pregnancy.

March 21, 2011

We told all the friends this weekend about the baby. Nehemiah seemed apprehensive about telling other people. We talked about it yesterday. He said he wants to tell everyone but is apprehensive because he is scared. That sucks that it's that way. I know its unavoidable, but it sucks.

March 22, 2011

Went to my first doctor's appointment Tuesday. I was disappointed and discouraged. I guess I was expecting more, and now he (Doctor) wants to check me for everything. I thought we already knew for sure I have APS. I was trying to feel calm about it, but after that I got worried. Everything is fine so far, and they will watch us very carefully. I guess I will worry until I have the baby. I just feel weird; I can't even explain it. I feel like its surreal. Does that mean a part of me knows it's not going to happen? Or is a part of me just tripping out that I am going to really have a baby this time? AHHHH! I don't know. I do know that I 100% want to enjoy this pregnancy. Even just saying that makes me feel better. Being pregnant is great. This time will be watched super close. I will do kick counts all the time. It is happening this time!!!!! I think so. I just need to put those worries in God's hands. I really am trying to do just that. Lord, please help us to have a healthy baby, please. Help me to enjoy the pregnancy and to not be stressed.

Again, I did what I had with Bishop. I ate right and got plenty of rest. I also gained a fun little addition of anxiety and fear to my daily regimen. I spent hours researching my diagnosis. I read countless message boards looking for a mirror of myself that would give me peace of mind. I wrote down statistics and read scientific papers about different treatments. I searched and searched for a magic bullet to bring me peace of mind. However, despite the searching, I never found the magic bullet. (Spoiler alert: you can't find peace of that nature on a message board or in statistics.)

During this pregnancy, I was still going through the process of grief. I was still reeling from the loss of Bishop. I was still obsessively placing the urn in the safe when I left the house. I was still ashamed to talk about losing Bishop. I was still wracked with guilt about failing him and more guilt for moving forward with my life. Endless circular thoughts filled my mind. Is it too soon to get pregnant again? Am I not honoring Bishop's memory? Will my marriage be damaged if this fails again? Is it worth the risk right now when our hearts are not in a good place? Now that I was pregnant, I had to fight the fear. I was constantly scared of hurting the baby or losing the baby. In addition, I still had fears of not loving the baby, of not being the mother this baby deserved.

March 28, 2011

So, I am a bit worried that I won't love this baby the way I loved Bishop. I'm worried my heart won't do it. I just want to make sure I am the mommy I truly want to be. I want her/him to feel loved, protected, all that. I'm just afraid I won't bond with her/him. I know it happens to some women. They don't bond with the child-like a kind of postpartum depression, I guess. That would be awful. I want to be close to this baby. When I was pregnant with Bishop, I was so sure. This is all so confusing.

With my previous pregnancy ending in stillbirth, we were considered a high-risk pregnancy. As such, my level of medical care was much more significant during this pregnancy. With that in mind, I felt better but still anxious about the physical aspects of the pregnancy. I was calmer than I would have been had I not been watched closely by our doctors. Early in the pregnancy the doctor did every test imaginable.

March 29, 2011

Yesterday, the doctor called to let me know that my progesterone levels were low (5). Normal levels are 15. So, I had to go buy some medicine. I was really upset. I just want to have a baby.

What if?

Please, God, let me have a baby.

The doctor said low progesterone is not that uncommon, and I was reassured I could take medicine to overcome the problem quickly. Thankfully, I took the medicine and my levels returned to normal. Even though everything seemed fine with the baby, I paid extra close attention to any changes in my body. Any little change in how I felt would invoke a new anxiety.

March 31, 2011

Last night my nausea got a little better and this morning I didn't feel like I would be sick. To be honest this scared me, that maybe not feeling sick is a bad sign. I knew I would feel this way if I got pregnant again. This is all because the day before we lost Bishop, I felt like I could breathe easier and I was relieved. But come to find out, I could breathe easier because he was dying. So, I am gun-shy. I really don't want to feel this way the entire time I am pregnant. I want to enjoy the experience. I am really trying not to worry about those things. I am doing absolutely everything that can be done right now.

The day before we lost Bishop a couple of things happened that seemed significant after we lost him. First, I lost a couple of pounds. Second, I could breathe easier. Losing a couple pounds could be attributed to the water level in my uterus lowering a bit because he had died. Being able to breathe easier was because he shifted lower into the birth canal. According to my doctor this was because the baby had died, and my body was already going through the physical process of ridding my body of his. After experiencing those symptoms, I was hyper vigilant to any changes in my body. I weighed myself most mornings, and I constantly researched any and every symptom to see if it were an indication of miscarriage.

In April, I began seeing a high-risk pregnancy doctor. It was this doctor who would give the "magic medicine bullet" to having a healthy baby. He prescribed 40 mg of blood thinner injections and a baby aspirin every day for the duration of my pregnancy. From all the research I had been doing, I was familiar with the success rate of this regimen in APS pregnancies. We began administering injections every evening. We would pinch a little fat on my stomach and inject the medicine. Occasionally, we would hit a blood vessel, and it would leave a bruise, or occasionally the medicine would sting going in. I was assured every time we plunged that medicine into my stomach that we were doing everything to avoid a repeat of last year. Our pregnancy continued well but with some scary moments.

I'm Scared

As my pregnancy progressed, I maintained my hyper vigilance in monitoring the baby and my physical conditions. Any irregularity (or perceived irregularity) ended in a call to the doctor. In June, I had a bad bleeding episode.

June 3, 2011

A few days ago, we had a bad bleeding episode. I ended up going to the emergency room. The baby is ok, thank God. I really thought we had lost the baby, but thank God the baby is fine. I have been using a heart rate monitor daily, and the baby has been very active. I have fallen for him (pretty sure I saw a penis in the ultrasound the other day). I was afraid to do that; it scares me to get attached. A large part of me thinks that everything will be alright. I will be scared until he is in my arms, and then I am sure I will find new things to worry about. Please, Lord, bless us with a healthy baby.

I remember when the bleeding started, my heart sank. My only thought in those first moments before we went to the emergency room was, "*We lost this baby, too.*" On the way to the hospital, I remember mentally preparing for the bad news I was sure was coming. This was it, the moment I had feared. The hospital took us back rather quickly to the ultrasound machines. We found ourselves back in the same place where we were told Bishop had died. It felt like a rerun. Wasn't I just here? Now here we were waiting to be told our second child had died, too. Or so I thought…

They got me all situated for an ultrasound, and there it was… a heartbeat. I remember being surprised seeing the heartbeat on the monitor. I had assumed the absolute worst, but the baby was fine. I had passed a large blood clot that was probably on the outside of my placenta. The baby's heart rate was good; everything checked out. I was put on bed rest for a few days, and they sent us on our way.

In response to the bleeding episode, my doctor lowered my blood thinners to 30 mg. A logical response to bleeding is to reduce the blood thinners. All the research I had read, though, said the "magic medicine bullet" was 40 mg, so I was wracked with anxiety that the baby wasn't getting the blood needed to develop properly, and we would miscarry. I was scared the doctors were making a mistake.

June 6, 2011

I have been worrying about my weight lately. When we lost Bishop, I had lost a few pounds in the days leading up to his death. So now I'm watching my weight like a hawk, just in case. I need to get a digital scale to make me feel better. I just want to have a healthy baby. I keep wishing I had some kind of guarantee, some way of knowing all will be ok. All I have is hope. Sometimes that doesn't seem to be enough. I feel like I need to be able to catch any problems. But I am not psychic. I know I am not, but I still feel like I need to be able to save this baby because I didn't save Bishop. Even though I don't blame myself for that... but maybe I do.

After a couple of weeks at the lower blood thinner dosage, the specialist returned me to the regular dosage. I was relieved to be back at the 40 mg. Still, though, the fear I was battling controlled most of my days. I started my days anxious about the urn. Then continued my day with other obsessions.

I wore a bracelet in this season, made by a dear friend, with Bishop's initials on it. It was a beautiful gift. This beautiful gift turned into an obsession. If the clasp of the bracelet was not facing the correct direction, I worried God would be mad, and we would lose the baby. As soon as I would realize the bracelet was turned, I would immediately correct it. I would then begin to pray, asking God for forgiveness and to give us a healthy baby.

Looking back at this, what strikes me is that this obsession seemed logical. It was all about control. If I controlled the entire day to make sure every tiny detail was perfect, then God would bless us with a healthy baby. I cried out prayers of grace, forgiveness, and mercy often, daily, every minute. Not out of a place of worship or dedication, but out of a need for control. Surely, if I talked to God often enough, I could control the outcome of this pregnancy. Surely, if I were "enough" this time around, we could have a healthy baby. Maybe last time I just had not prayed enough, hadn't been enough for God's favor to shine on Bishop. Maybe I could turn that around this time by doing everything I could to please God, including making sure my bracelet was facing the right direction. It all boiled down to control. Control born of fear.

I stated at the beginning of this book that I have written this for you, but in this moment of pouring out my heart, I see that this book was as much about my healing as it is about yours. Until this moment, I had not seen this obsession for what it was. I was working to gain the grace of God on my life. (Spoiler alert: I already had it; Jesus got it for me.) I didn't enjoy my time at the feet of Jesus. Instead, I came to His feet full of dread, scared of His wrath, a wrath I kept trying to avoid through obsessions.

June 29, 2011

I am an emotional mess today. I am worried about the baby and I miss Bishop. Being a mommy is hard. I never got to really love on Bishop. He was decomposing, his skin was sticky, he would even bleed at times. Lord, please don't let that happen to this baby. I really want a healthy baby. My Bishop was beautiful. Please bless us with another beautiful son, but one who is healthy. I know the baby is active right now and all looks good for now, but after my appointment yesterday with the specialist, I am worried that the blood thinner isn't enough, that the baby will struggle just like Bishop. I feel like we will have a live baby this time, but I am worried he will have health problems. I am trying to stay calm. I don't want to raise my blood pressure. I wish there was a way of knowing if we are doing everything we can, but all we can do is wait. However, then it could be too late. Yesterday the doctor said that if this pregnancy doesn't work, then we will know next time I need more blood thinners. I don't want to admit it to Nehemiah, but I don't think I could do this again. If we lose this baby like we lost Bishop, I don't think I can try again. Lord, please don't let that happen. He is so great right now. Active and growing at least 2 ounces a week. He is 12 ounces this week, which is fantastic, and I feel him move quite often now. I'm scared. All I can do is wait. I know that aggravates the controlling part of me. God is in control I know, but I still worry I am not doing enough.

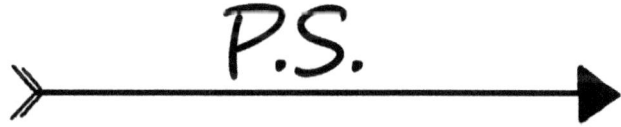

"I keep wishing I had some kind of guarantee."
Don't we all.
I know since that day in January 2010 when I found out I was pregnant with Bishop, I have thought many times how much easier life would be with all the answers to the future in front of me. If only I had a guarantee that things would go well. If only I knew for sure my heart would not be crushed. If only, if only. I am sure you have felt this way before. We are not guaranteed tomorrow, but we are given faith and hope. Do not be discouraged, my friends; lean on faith. Know that God has great plans to prosper you. He will not forsake you. He does have all the answers to the future in front of Him, so rest in the knowledge you are guaranteed. He will take care of you.

Anniversary or Birthday?

The anniversary of losing Bishop loomed, and we wanted to honor it somehow, not with just sadness. We decided to make grief kits to hand out to local hospitals. Each kit contained a journal, a card from the Women's Resource Center, and an angel keepsake. I knew writing in my journals had helped me. I hoped it would help others. Looking back on my journals, I see so often my attempts at comforting myself. In July I wrote a quote from Ruth Bell Graham which reads, "As a mother, my job is to take care of what is possible and trust God with the impossible." Trust… the elusive piece of this puzzle I could not find in my season of grief and loss.

August 2, 2011

In a few days it will be the anniversary of the loss of my Bishop. I'm not sure what to call this day. Nehemiah says we should call it his birthday because I gave birth to him. But he lost his life before that, so I don't know. I guess it really doesn't matter, it is just a label, it doesn't change what it is. Nehemiah and I are going to finish the grief kits this week to give away to the local hospitals. I pray they bring someone some peace.

In a couple of weeks, I will be in that pregnancy window where Bishop started to struggle. I am nervous about it. I just pray October gets here quickly. I want to have a healthy baby desperately.

Lord, please bless me with a sense of calm over the next 10 or so weeks and give me strength to wait patiently. Please put your hand on our baby and keep him safe and healthy. Thank you for all your blessings and all your blessings to come. Amen.

August 4, 2011

Today, a year ago, I was blissfully pregnant with my Bishop and had no worries. He may have died this day or tomorrow, I am not sure. He had been moving so little. I guess for the rest of my life I will grieve for the birthday parties we will never have, the 1st birthday kisses, the first cake.

I had to stop writing for a while; I am emotional today. I couldn't stop crying. I don't want to upset the baby; he is my number 1 priority. I miss my Bishop terribly today and am sad about the loss of his precious baby moments that we never get to expe-

rience. This baby in my belly is going to town, moving around, reminding me to be strong and positive.

Bishop's birthday came and went. We donated the grief kits to the hospitals, and I survived the pain of that day. There were several pivotal moments in my grief journey. I worried over these moments for weeks leading up to them; I had made myself a wreck long before they came. A couple of pivotal moments that come to mind: our due date, going to work, going to the pool, and his birthday. As I discovered with them all, the buildup is worse. I would work myself up with anxiety, and then it was nowhere near as bad as I had anticipated.

Another pivotal moment was the point in my first pregnancy when Bishop died, thirty-two weeks. I would be thirty-two weeks into this second pregnancy soon, and I couldn't help but consider the scary reality of history repeating itself.

September 9, 2011

This is the time when I lost Bishop last pregnancy. A part of me can't shake the lingering feeling of nervousness about that. The baby is active and showing nothing but good signs. So, I should be comforted by that, which I am, but still. I just can't wait to have the baby. It's not too long now, only 5 weeks till full term; 7 weeks till the absolute end. I am hoping I will have the baby the week of Halloween. It would be fun to have spooky dress up birthday parties.

The baby continued to have good test results. I continued to monitor the movements, and the baby continued to grow.

October 3, 2011

October is finally here. This could be the month I have the baby. No more than 4 weeks, not counting this week. The baby is measuring at 37 weeks last week so maybe I will labor early. I am getting uneasy about the labor part. What if I go into labor fast and the baby is stressed? I am just unprepared, I guess. I don't know what to expect. I'm super excited. September went by fast so hopefully October will go by even faster. Please, God, keep us safe for this last month and see us through a safe delivery.

It's a Boy

On that morning in late October, I woke with a heart full of nervousness. The baby didn't seem to be moving much, and I began to get scared. What if the baby is dying in my belly again? I called my mom, and she took me to the hospital to be monitored. This was a regular trip for me. I went to the doctor to check on the baby a lot. Fortunately, the baby was doing fine (breech position but good heart rate). We were sent home. Once home, I lay down for a nap. I woke from my nap around four o'clock in the afternoon. As soon as I stood up from the bed, my water broke. The baby was coming.

We welcomed our second son to the world at 6:58 p.m. via C-section (because he was breech).

November 9, 2011

> *Here we are on the other side of an exceptionally long and trying journey. Baby is here. We made it. The blood thinners worked. Thank God. He is beautiful. Nehemiah is a super Dad. He is so hands-on and loves to be involved. We are very blessed. I must admit I was worried about something happening to the baby, but I think that is just because I have never felt this strongly about anyone before. So, I worry about him. I have relaxed some. I know we are doing everything we can do to protect him. He is healthy and wonderful. God, please keep my family safe and happy. Thank you for all the blessings; the baby is truly a gift from you. Thank you. Thank you.*

We were thrilled to welcome our second son. I recovered relatively easily, and we began our life as a family of three. Being a mother is an amazing experience, and getting to hold our son alive and well was beyond my imagination.

Even though the baby had been delivered safely, I was fearful something would happen to him. I remember being afraid to go home from the hospital because we did not have armed security at home. What if someone broke in and stole him? I always wanted to be touching him to calm my fears. We put his crib in our room on my side of the bed. He was literally two feet from me. Even this distance brought on anxiety. What if someone broke in and got between me and the baby? At my postpartum checkup, my doctor asked me if I had been having any mental struggles, to which I answered

honestly. To my surprise this was a common occurrence for postpartum, and it usually lessened six weeks after delivery. For me, the intensity of the anxiety did lessen to my "normal" dull roar after several weeks.

The family of three

Church Home

I didn't write in my journal much during 2012. Being a new mom kept me preoccupied. I functioned as a wife and new mom. Although motherhood consumed most of my thought process, I was still grieving. My battles with guilt, shame, fear, and anxiety continued. I wasn't crying all day, but those deep-rooted unresolved issues were manifesting in the form of jealousy, anger, insecurity, pride, and an overwhelming desire to prove myself worthy (which is just pride in reverse, if you think about it). I was plain uncomfortable and insecure in my own skin. I did not see myself as worthy. I saw myself as a failure with a fake façade of "success." I worked tirelessly to make sure no one really understood how I felt about myself.

Near the end of 2012, Nehemiah and I began discussing going to church regularly. Nehemiah had spent a lot of his youth in church and understood the value of church family. I had been a sporadic church goer. I would go occasionally when visiting my grandparents or Dad. My grandparents had the same home church for many years. Their love of Christ had spoken to my heart since I was young. They were always so peaceful and joyful. We knew we wanted that peace within our family. The only problem was, I was nervous to leave our son in the nursery. To begin our search, I started scouting churches while Nehemiah stayed home with the baby. In January 2013, we attended Northwood Church in Gulfport, Miss., for the first time. Northwood was a church like none other I had ever experienced. There were large TV screens showing song lyrics, people worshiping with their hands lifted into the air. To be honest, I was a bit taken aback; it was so loud and bright. Was this the church for us? Despite my apprehension, after service I checked out the nursery. The volunteer staff gave me a tour and explained their cleaning routine and safety protocols. I left that day feeling like I might be comfortable enough to leave our son in the nursery for an hour or so. I went home and told Nehemiah. We attended as a family the following week. Again, I was a bit taken aback by the bright lights and people raising their hands in worship; I just was not sure. Nehemiah was, though; he loved it. He knew this was the place for us. We began attending Northwood regularly. This was the single most influential decision of my life; it completely changed our trajectory.

Making the commitment to attend regular church services changed our lives for the better in many ways. Nehemiah and I agree that the reason for the peace our family currently is blessed with is because of this one decision we made in 2013, a decision made because we wanted something better for our family. However, I didn't realize how much I needed something better. I could never have imagined the healing and discovery that God had in store for us. I am so grateful for Nehemiah and his leadership of our family in choosing Northwood as our home.

Power of Prayer

During those early months at Northwood Church, I remember feeling out of place, not because the people were uninviting, but because in my heart, I felt I was not one of them. I had some serious doubts. I believed in God, a higher power, if you will. Everything else, though, made no sense to me. I wasn't sure I believed any of it. I would stand during worship filled with envy of the people who lifted their hands in surrendered devotion. They worshiped with such abandon and faith. They seemed so sure of their chosen status, so sure that Jesus had come and died for them. To me they were so beautiful in those moments of faith-filled joy.

Several Sundays, I wished I could believe in my heart that Jesus came and died for me, that I had a Savior who loved me enough to die on a cross and cover me in his cleansing blood. A large part of me wanted to believe. I wanted the peace I had witnessed in others. I wanted relief from the thoughts of failure and fear that surrounded me daily. I wanted to be chosen. But it seemed out of reach for me. I thought I would never be worthy of salvation. The list of reasons why I could never be in the group with these beautiful devotees seemed long and detailed. For starters, I had failed to keep my son alive. I should have known something was wrong with him and saved him. Second, I operated daily in selfish ambition to convince others I was good enough, and I was ruled by fearful thoughts that controlled daily life. Most importantly, I really wasn't sure I believed in Jesus, anyway. That seemed like an automatic disqualification. I could never be worthy to be one of these faith-filled, joyful devotees.

For months we went; for months I listened; I took notes; I read scriptures after service. I stood during worship and awed at the people freely worshiping. Despite all this, my heart stayed hardened until one Sunday when God pricked me in the one tiny crack my hardened heart had.

It was Father's Day, June 9, 2013. We went to church like we had been doing for the last several months. While the lead pastor preached, the presence of God came over me, and I began to cry. I could not stop the tears; for a good hour or so they poured down my face. I was a complete mess, so I had to make my way to the restroom to clean my face. On my way, I passed the leader of the church nursery. Seeing my distress, she followed me into the restroom to check on me. Through my sobs and tears, I told her the whole story about losing Bishop and the guilt of failing him. I explained how I should have known that he was in distress and that I was ashamed of failing as his mother. This woman who barely knew me stood in that bathroom with me and listened. She didn't have a look of shock on her face. She never once looked at me with those "knowing" eyes that said I had killed my son with my "toxic" uterus. She didn't recoil from me as if I had a mark that said, "bad mom." She listened. Then she took my hands and prayed with me in the middle of the bathroom. She spoke a prayer over my life that Jesus would heal my heart. She prayed to the Savior that she knew could place my heart in the right place to receive healing, the healing she knew was available to me because she knew Jesus had given his blood for me to have it. This is the moment that Jesus began my healing journey. This is the moment God began to reconstruct my heart and heal me from the pain I had carried for years.

June 18, 2013

On June 9, 2013 we went to Church. The pastor preached about pride and how, to think you are above God, is a sin. This message really affected me. I broke down. I couldn't stop crying. I think this all related to me still having feelings of guilt about Bishop. I thought I had forgiven myself, but I guess not. I hadn't truly given it to God and got rid of it from my heart. I asked for the Lord to take it from my heart. I know it worked. I no longer feel as weighed down by my guilt. I didn't realize it was so heavy on me. But God knows what we need. He knew I needed to truly lay that at His feet. Maybe I can lay it down totally.

It had been almost three years since we lost Bishop. I had been on the roller coaster of grief for three long years. Battling to understand, battling to breathe, battling to smile. I had been carrying around heavy burdens of guilt, shame, fear, and anxiety, burdens that were binding me and preventing me from living a life of freedom -- the life Jesus calls all of us to live.

I didn't realize how significant that moment at church in June was for me. I didn't fully realize what happened. I just knew something significant had happened, and it was probably God. When I left church on that Sunday, the sky had not changed color, and I had not magically forgotten all my issues. It was not a light-switch type of situation. What did happen on that day was I met hope, a hope I didn't know I needed, a hope I didn't know was possible. I knew God had spoken hope to my hardened heart that day. I knew that there was a lot more I didn't know… a lot. But I was determined to find out more.

PART 4

The Reconstruction

Serving

After my experience with the healing power of prayer at church that day in June, I began actively seeking God. It was one of those rare moments in life when you "know in your knower" there is more in store for you. I knew the experience I had on Father's Day was just the tip of the iceberg. The Bible says that if you seek God, you will find Him (Deuteronomy 4:29), and let me tell you, friends, it's true! God immediately got to work on my heart! He came in strong to heal the battles of guilt, anxiety, shame, and fear that I had been fighting for years. Over the next six years, God showed me my life could be full of hope, faith, love, and grace abounding.

After the beginning stages of denial and anger, I began my struggle with guilt. It was this guilt that God healed. The key to healing my guilt was to forgive myself. To do that I needed the realization that I was worthy of forgiveness. To do this, I had to get to know the one who forgave first: Jesus. I thought I knew. I went to Sunday school occasionally, vacation Bible school in the summer sometimes; surely, I had the knowledge, right? Wrong.

If I were to summarize my thoughts on God leading up to this point in my life, I would say I knew *of* God. He existed. He created life. He would get mad and punish people, and most importantly, I knew I had to accept Jesus to avoid hell when I died. Noticeably, these are all religious things. The take home packet of faith, if you will (a packet missing some leaflets, surely). I had, what you would call the worldly view of Christianity. I had been worried about going to hell, so I did the things I thought ensured that I would not have to worry about going to hell.

In August 2013, I started serving in the church nursery. Now, you are probably assuming it was because I wanted to give back some of the love I had felt the day God touched my heart. Well… it wasn't. My main motivation was guilt. I felt guilty (here we go again with the guilt) for taking advantage of the nursery services provided by the church and not contributing. So, to quiet the little voice of guilt in my mind, I began serving. I started in the infant room. I would hold, rock, change, and enjoy the babies while serving alongside other women.

I served alongside women who had been in the church their entire lives, women with solid Christian faith, women I was sure I would never measure up against. I mean, they had this faith thing nailed down. I, on the other hand, was still not sure what I believed. I was afraid these women would discover that I was a fraud. Surely, any minute, I would get the boot. I knew I was not in the "club," nor would I ever be. I knew God had spoken to my heart, but I still was not sure what I believed. Was Jesus even real?

    Despite my doubts, I kept serving and started to get to know the ladies. I began making friends, and these women began to share their testimonies with me. They shared how God had moved in their lives. I got to see, over and over, how God loved each of these women as a daughter. He had impacted their lives in amazing ways. None of the stories were exactly like mine, but despite the differences, I realized these Christian women were just like me. They were flawed; they had doubts; they feared they were failing their families; they struggled with mom guilt; they were trying to nail down this faith thing the same as me. These women would listen when I needed to talk or talk when I needed to listen. I learned so much about being a woman from these ladies. Again, I had a "know in my knower" type of moment and knew that serving was part of the process God had created for me to get to know Him better.

    Through serving, I discovered that God wants a relationship with us. God loves us and cares about each of us as His children. Through serving I discovered that I could be part of the family of God. After that realization, I began to say yes to any other church service opportunities that came my way.

Healed from Guilt

As we continued to attend church and serve, God continued to place opportunities for our family to learn His character and heart for us. Nehemiah and I attended a small group with our pastor, and we developed relationships as a couple. Nehemiah began serving on the parking lot team. I began running with several ladies from church on Saturday mornings. As a family, we grew closer to the church and the family of Christ. I continued to read my Bible and continued searching for understanding. A year or so after my "run in" with God on Father's Day, I found myself wrestling with faith in Jesus Christ as my Savior. I knew that, over the past year, God had been working on my heart, but I just couldn't shake my doubt in Jesus.

Every Sunday in church, I would watch the other worshipers lift their hands and sing. They seemed so joyful and peaceful. I was jealous of their seemingly strong faith. How did they lift their hands with such abandon? How were they so sure that the Jesus we were singing about was real and died for their sins? Why can't I lift my hands in trust and worship? *How do I get there?* I just couldn't wrap my heart and my mind around it. Every week, during the invitation, I would ask Jesus to come into my heart, and every week I would hold my heart back.

I adopted an approach where I would visualize a door on my heart, then I would kick doors down and invite Jesus in. Despite this visualization, I still held my heart back. Why was I struggling with this so much? I was frustrated with myself and my lack of faith.

One day while I was driving to work, all the doubt came to a head. I remember the moment very clearly. I had been struggling that week with the idea of Jesus. I kept replaying in my mind all the moments over the past years when I knew God had been working in my life. I thought back to the moments I knew could not have been possible. I knew that I wouldn't have been functioning had God not stepped into my life. Looking back, I could see I needed help, and God had stepped in.

My heart filled with a peace I had not experienced before. Then I had a moment of clarity. I knew that there was no way that the God moments I had experienced over the past year would have happened if I hadn't had a Savior. No way was I worthy of that kind of love and grace. No way was I important enough for the creator of the world to take an interest in me. Why would God bother with me *unless* I had a Savior in Jesus -- a Savior who came before me to pave the way for me to receive the healing power of God. I decided that day, in my car, to never again doubt Jesus. I knew that Jesus died for me to cover my sins so that I, an imperfect sinner, could experience the grace and healing power of God. In short, no way God would *choose* me if Jesus had not chosen me first. I have never again doubted my Jesus's love or sacrifice for me.

With the realization that Jesus forgave me and washed me clean, I was able to begin forgiving myself. I laid the guilt from failing Bishop at Jesus's feet. Now, friends, I will not lie to you and say that the thoughts of guilt do not try to creep up on me. They do. In the beginning, I had to make a daily choice and continue forgiving and laying it down. I had to *choose* to forgive myself. I had to choose to see me the way Jesus sees me, clean and worthy of forgiveness. I was finally able to accept that Bishop's death was the result of an undiagnosed medical condition that I had no idea about. I was not a bad mother. It was not my fault. Friends, choose to forgive, because Jesus died for that forgiveness.

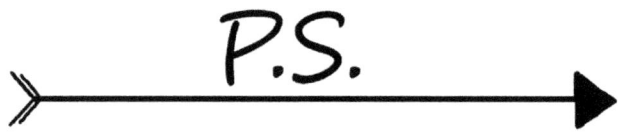

That moment in my car is what I have heard called my "elevator" salvation story. It is a quick salvation story to tell someone when you only have two minutes to share about Jesus.

What is your "elevator" salvation story?

Baby #3

In 2014, Nehemiah and I decided to try again for another baby. I began tracking my ovulation and keeping records. In January 2015, the church did what they called a week of momentum to prepare for the new year. It was a week spent in fasting, prayer, and nightly worship services. Nehemiah and I joined in and focused our prayers on expanding our family. We fasted, prayed, and worshiped alongside our church family.

January 5, 2015

Prayer needs: Pray for increase for our family -- new baby

Three months later we found out that we were expecting. I looked back at my ovulation calendar, and it was the weekend of that fast that God blessed us with our third child. No one could ever convince me that prayer and fasting do not work.

This pregnancy was much easier for several reasons: I knew the medicine worked, and I was walking with God. I no longer stressed about the state of the clasp on my bracelet. No longer did I think I needed to gain the favor of God to save my child. I knew I was a daughter of Christ. I knew.

During my third pregnancy, I fought hard for the rest provided in God's provision and plan. I was able to give thanks to God for the life growing inside of me and enjoy the experience. I was not waking in the night looking for ways to control the outcome. I prayed and stayed in contact with God. I enjoyed the sensation of our child kicking and growing. I no longer faced the days with worry. One could assume that many factors besides my faith made a difference in my mental state during this pregnancy. These include the length of time since Bishop's death, delivering a healthy baby once already, age, wisdom… the list can go on. I am sure these factors had an impact, but I am also sure that without the spark of hope that I experienced in June 2013, I would not have been in a place to receive any of them in a positive way.

Our first picture as a family of four

On October 3, 2015, at 5:00 a.m., we welcomed our third child into the world. I remember, after his birth, I was blown away at the blessings given to our family. Just five years earlier I had questioned whether we would have any children, and here we were with two healthy, happy babies. God is so good!

Healed from Shame

We settled in with our new family of four and continued to attend church and serve. I had decided to say yes to any service roles presented to me, and with that decision came several new roles at church. I stayed in the nursery realm, but I was asked to take on more leadership roles. This was an intimidating challenge, but I truly felt that saying yes to service opportunities was what God wanted me to do. I knew I had learned so much about God's love for me while serving, so, I began leading ladies. At one point, I shared my reasonings about why I said yes with one of my pastors. He suggested I share my story with the church by allowing them to make a video testimonial.

This request sent up red flags of shame immediately. As I said, I had begun to lay down the guilt, but the shame was different. Guilt said I did something wrong. Shame said I was the something wrong. The shame I felt after losing Bishop reared its ugly head. This shame had caused me to avoid places where people might ask me questions. I felt that the pastor wanted me to tell all the mothers in the room that I had failed as a mother. He wanted me to admit to a large crowd that I was incapable of taking care of my child like he deserved. I was nervous. Could I do that? Would the women I served alongside see me differently if they knew? I had shared the story with some of the women I was closer with, but to a room full of people, could I do that? I even had a thought that all the pregnant women in the room would be afraid of me, like I carried a contagious virus or something. Do not touch that lady; her son died at thirty-two weeks; you might get it on you and experience the same thing. I played all the scenarios of *rejection* over and over in my head. Despite the apprehension, I kept mulling it over. Could I do it? Would it help someone?

I spoke to Nehemiah about the request and he thought it was a good idea. He thought that maybe it would help someone. He thought maybe it would lead someone to find healing. I wasn't sure about that. I decided to fast and pray. After I spent several days praying and fasting, God laid it on my heart to go through with it. The church production folks came to my house and filmed me telling the whole story. It was not a long process, but my stomach was in knots the entire time. It aired August 2018, the weekend we would have celebrated Bishop's eighth birthday.

My stomach flipped as I sat by the people I had grown to love as they watched my failure spelled out in detail. The overwhelming shame I battled threatened to make me flee from the room. I knew people would look at me differently. I knew there would be those knowing eyes screaming that I had failed. I kept thinking people would be scared of me. Mothers would not want me near them. People would look at me differently, knowing that I could not do the biological thing women are made to do. The endless scenarios kept playing in my mind as I watched myself tell the story.

After the video was played, what I feared would happen did not happen. As a matter of fact, our story was well received. I have since had women approach me because they recognize me from the video, and I can share about the grace God extended to me. I have had the privilege to speak to many women since this time about their fertility struggles, women who harbor the same sense of failure I struggled with. Women far stronger than I.

I have discovered the loss of a pregnancy is something women hold deep in their hearts, something we struggle to speak about. I think we hold this sadness deep in our hearts for several reasons, the first being that it is a deep period of deep mourning no matter where you are in your pregnancy: first, second, or third trimester. For some reason though, it seems like people assume you will not mourn because you have not actually met that child. I do not know why. I have spoken to mothers who have apologized for being so upset. I have heard the, *"I know I was not that far along yet, but I just cannot stop being sad. I am so sorry."* My heart aches for these mothers who feel it is not okay to not be okay. If you are in this group of apologetic mourners, it is ok to grieve for the loss of your child. I know that God has a purpose for even the shortest of lives.

The second reason, the one that I am the most familiar with, is shame, the shame of not doing what we are made to do. We are women, biologically built to bring forth life. If a woman can't bear a child, there is a sense that there must be something wrong, something that we should be ashamed of. I was ashamed that I did not know something was wrong with Bishop. I cried many tears because I failed him as his mother. Even as I write this, I feel the failure tugging, whispering shame, this shame that isolated me for so long. It was in sharing the grace and love that had been given to me that shame was defeated. It was in sharing the hope and forgiveness I found with Jesus that I walked away from the shame.

Healed from Anxiety

Early in my grief, I began battling anxieties as a side effect of the pain and guilt. I would make myself sick with anxiety. I constantly worried about something happening to my family. I constantly feared loss or disappointing my husband or not being enough for my family. I remember lying awake at night, running scenarios over in my mind about bad things happening. Sometimes I would think about good things that happened but overanalyze how other people viewed them. I constantly worried about what other people were thinking. Then there were nights I was convinced my family and I would not be alive in the morning; I just knew something would happen to us – a fire, a burglar, a tsunami … the list went on and on. Even hearing planes fly over the house would elicit anxious fears of its falling on our heads and killing us. I struggled to sleep sometimes because of the "what ifs" endlessly circling my mind. I struggled to travel with work away from my family because of feeling that something would happen to them. These anxieties bothered me, of course, but I considered them to be normal. I assumed it was part of who I was. I just assumed I was an anxious person.

With the realization that Christ died for me to wash away all my sins came the realization that He died so I could live life abundantly. Was I living life abundantly? Was this constant companion of anxiety impeding the life God had designed for me? Yes … it was. Could God heal this in me, too? I was not sure. Aren't these normal parts of life? Isn't this just part of who I am?

I began to question this anxious, fearful normalcy several years ago. I began my offensive attack against these circular, anxious thoughts by fighting with prayer and simply speaking the name of Jesus into the darkness of the night when my mind would spin. I admit, I began the offense of prayer with doubt. Anxiety seemed as if it were part of my person. I held tightly to the thought of anxiety being a part of who I was. I even had family members tell me that it was just something I did. It was a defining part of my character, a defining part that I had allowed to be stuck to me.

In 2019, Nehemiah and I signed up for freedom groups at our church. This 12-week program is designed to expand your knowledge of the love of God so you can lay your chains at the feet of Jesus and find freedom. During this program, I shared with my ladies' group about the anxiety I had been fighting for years and how it had been affecting me when traveling for work, affecting me to the point of breakdowns about something happening to my family when I was away on business. The group prayed over me, and one of the ladies said that God told her I needed to find the root of this anxiety. I had never thought about this before. Was there a root? Could this pit in my stomach really have a starting place?

It was then that I remembered about Bishop's urn and how I felt that day when I was afraid to leave my house for fear of something happening to the urn in my absence. I thought about how I had chosen to leave the house that day despite my fears. I thought I had defeated that anxiety, but I had defeated only one anxiety in that one moment. The anxiety I was letting infiltrate my daily life was the same as not wanting to leave the house. They were packaged differently, but they were essentially the same. Again, I had to make a choice to leave the house and lay down the anxiety.

October 27, 2019

I am going out of town again for a week for work. When I go out of town, the anxiety rises. I had several scary dreams last night. My stomach is in knots. I know these work trips are helping my career. I know my family is safe. Why do I feel so anxious and scared?

October 28, 2019

Is the anxiety I feel rooted in losing Bishop and being afraid I will lose my family? Do I trust God with my family? I guess not, honestly, I mean, look at Bishop. But I know Bishop had a purpose. My sons have a purpose. I need to rest knowing God has them on a path only He controls. Having these doubts makes me ashamed. Uggh, here we go again with the shame. Why? Why can't I trust?

I knew I needed to lay this anxiety down, so on that same day, on that same page, in my journal, I prayed.

Lord God, help me to overcome this anxiety! I claim victory! I claim freedom! I claim rest in knowing you are in control! In Jesus's name, Amen.

Now, as I write this, it doesn't escape me that it sounds too good to be true. Again, I am telling you I just decided to lay it down. For me, I prayed, and I gave the anxiety to Jesus. Anxiety still tries to creep into my life time and time again, but I have developed a strategy I will share with you. I talk to Nehemiah about it. I reach out to my sisters in Christ, and I sing a little song, a little song that goes something like this: "Nope, d'nope nope nope, nope, nope." Yep, lyrical gold, I know. As silly as it seems, I am immediately pulled out of the anxiety and find peace. It refocuses my mind.

So, yes, I am telling you that to overcome the biggest hurdles in my journey, I had to make a choice. I had to choose to trust in God. I still must make a choice to trust God with my anxious thoughts. I still have days when my anxiety creeps up on me. I think I always will. Remember to make a choice to claim your freedom in Jesus. Make the choice every day for as long as it takes to retrain your brain. The Bible says that our minds can be renewed (Romans 12:2). Make a choice to be renewed. Make it and live in that choice.

♩ ♫ ♩ *Nope, de, nope* ♩ ♫ ♩

Walk Free, My Friends

Looking back on my journey through grief, I can see all the steps that helped me through the stages of denial, anger, pain and guilt, depression and loneliness, reconstruction, and freedom.

Some of my healing steps:
- Counseling.
- Practicing self-care through journaling and running.
- Learning to be kind to myself and my healing heart.
- Joining a church.
- Learning God's character by reading the Bible.
- Building a relationship with God through serving.
- Building relationships with other followers of Christ.
- Accepting my salvation.
- Praying and fasting.
- Continuing to serve and saying Yes to opportunities.

Most importantly, I encourage you to make a choice to not be controlled by the battles that come into your life. Grief is a process that requires time and patience. However, there comes a time when the side effects of grief (in my case guilt, shame, anxiety, and fear) are battles that must be defeated. There will always be battles, and they will look different. Choose to lean on God. Let Him fight your battles. Lay them at the feet of Jesus and walk away. He will tell you how to beat them. Choose to sing. I give you permission to use my "nope" song. It works, trust me. There will be days you find the things you laid down in prayer prickling your brain. You might feel anxious about something. Refocus on Jesus and lay it down again. Lay it down as many times as you must.

When I got to the end of this book, it felt very anticlimactic. I wrestled with telling you that the battles were won without any bloodshed, without any fight scenes worthy of a Hollywood movie. The thing is, though, everything I told you was true.

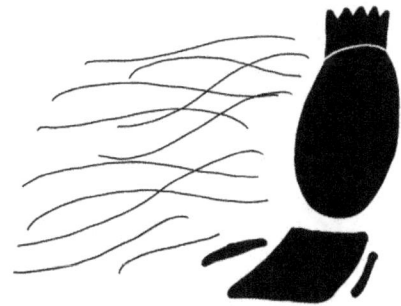

There were no Hollywood epic fight scenes involved in the making of this life (not a physical fight, anyway). I spoke to a dear friend about my concerns, and she helped me to figure out why. There is no epic fight scene, because that scene already happened. It happened when Jesus gave His life for us on the cross, when He sacrificed His sinless blood to save us. The battles have already been won, my friend. It is we who must reach out and grab hold of that victory, that truth. We must choose to walk in the freedom Jesus secured for us. It took me years to find my final stage of freedom. I pray each of you finds yours. Walk free, my friends, walk free.

www.ingramcontent.com/pod-product-compliance
Lightning Source LLC
LaVergne TN
LVHW051509070426
835507LV00022B/3010